HCD

Computer-Aided Marketing and Selling

Information Asset Management

Robert Shaw

Butterworth-Heinemann Ltd
Linacre House, Jordan Hill, Oxford OX2 8DP

 PART OF REED INTERNATIONAL BOOKS

OXFORD LONDON BOSTON
MUNICH NEW DELHI SINGAPORE SYDNEY
TOKYO TORONTO WELLINGTON

First published 1991

British Library Cataloguing in Publication Data
Shaw, Robert
  Computer-aided marketing and selling
  I. Title
  658.8

ISBN 0 7506 0070 5

Phototypeset by Key Graphics, Aldermaston, Berkshire
Printed in Great Britain by
Billing & Sons Ltd, Worcester

Contents

Preface

This book has two main aims. First, to help you understand how good (or bad) your company is at using information systems as Critical Success Factors in your marketing mix. Second, to help you create the right conditions for information systems to flourish and increase your marketing potential.

Part of this book is devoted to questionnaires. These are not given as a quiz, nor as some kind of complex technology test. Their purpose is solely to help you think through the factors that will enable you to make successful use of information systems in your own marketing and selling. I hope that your answers to these questions will provide valuable insights into your company. I am pretty sure that, if you are honest, some of your answers will embarrass you.

There also is a blueprint, showing how to construct successful systems. The book unravels and explains data applications and functional techniques, using simple terms to describe just what is meant by 'contact strategy', 'lifetime value', 'de-duplication', etc., and how they will affect the marketing organisation. A planning cycle is used to explore systematically the ways that marketing and selling will be affected by information systems.

However, the book is more about action than insights. All the management analysis and advice in the world is of little value if it does not lead to changes in behaviour, attitude and practice. Some of the questionnaires are action guides, which consist of logical sequences of questions to suggest practical steps that you can use to develop your own capabilities.

The book does not provide a guide to what resources are available – the reader is referred to Shaw Consulting's Sales and Marketing Systems Report or *DataPro*, which are the standard reference works, for that.

The book is written with four main groups of readers in view:

- marketing managers
- sales managers
- advertising agencies
- data processing managers and analysts.

Introduction – The Big IAM

You mentioned your name as if I should recognise it, but beyond the obvious facts that you are a bachelor, a solicitor, a freemason, and an asthmatic, I know nothing whatever about you.

It is a capital mistake to theorise before one has data.
    Sir Arthur Conan Doyle, The Memoirs of Sherlock Holmes (1892)

The essence of management thought has been widely reduced to a few Big Ideas: eight rules for excellence, seven Ss, six Ps, five competitive forces, four product life stages, three generic strategies and innumerable two-by-two matrices. But now, many managers are asking: 'Where do we go from here? Is there another Big Idea?'

The prevailing belief now is that the 'information society' is the important concept, and that by computerising information recording and analysis, people can create new wealth. Consequently, businesses have invested heavily in information technology. Today, more than $50 billion – roughly a third of all business capital expenditure in the USA – is earmarked for information technology. In the UK the situation is similar.

However, the link between information technology and profit has not always been clear. Indeed many contemporary management best-sellers say a great deal about the importance of information, but are curiously silent on the practical questions of how to turn information into wealth and how to manage one's information assets.

My earlier book, *Database Marketing*, was one of the first attempts to answer these questions. It explains how to create profitable demand from base information, within the confines of direct marketing.

Since its publication, the term 'database marketing' has become commonplace, and its application a growing part of the marketing mix. However, while database marketing has the fervent support of direct marketers, many people in general marketing and sales management are still failing dismally to capitalise on information technology.

They just seem to ignore the vast wealth of base sales and marketing data available from retail scanners, direct marketing, order processing, financial services, enquiries, coupons, sales visits, trade directories and public databases.

This book explains what is wrong, and shows what can be done about it. It reduces the problems and complexities to one big idea: *Information Asset Management* (the big IAM). It introduces the concept of information as an asset, and investigates the likely objectives and advantages of treating it as such.

INFORMATION ASSET MANAGEMENT

Why do companies fail to exploit information effectively? The answer is simply that managers do not appreciate the value of information and the need to manage it.

The problem is an organisational one, not a technical one. Thus it can only be rectified at the highest levels within the company. Yet in most companies today it is being tackled by technical staff and middle managers.

So, what information is important to your business, and why do you need to manage it?

- Who are your competitors and what are they doing?
- Who are your potential customers and what do they want?
- Where is that file if your secretary is off sick?

If you have such information, it will improve your speed, efficiency and effectiveness. But only if you manage it correctly. You need to know where it is, how to get at it and what to do with it. You must also be confident that the information is correct and up to date.

Information is a valuable possession, so valuable that it should be considered an asset. Let me illustrate.

CASE EXAMPLE – INFORMATION ASSET MANAGEMENT

A company was selling a small, insignificant brand of consumer product in the late 1970s. They needed to find the four million prospective customers for their 10 cent product, somewhere in the United States, a country whose population exceeds 250 million.

They succeeded. Through Information Asset Management they made a very good impression with their customers, who kept coming back over and over again, spending on average $1000 on repeat purchases of the product. They experienced 40 per cent compound annual growth, and gained 10 points market share over formidable opposition.

The company was Kimberly-Clark, and their product was Huggies – a disposable nappy.

They took the drastic decision to spend $10 million dollars on constructing a database programme to acquire, store and manage information about 75 per cent of the four million new mothers each year.

They start by getting the name of the expectant mother from the hospital or doctor. They then send the mother very personal letters, which include beautifully prepared educational pamphlets about caring for a new baby – communication that builds up a positive relationship with the mother. When she returns home with her baby, and needs diapers, Huggies cents-off coupons arrive, to cash in on the goodwill created by the pamphlets.

Furthermore, Kimberly-Clark created an invaluable by-product – a huge and continually growing database of information about parents and children. This database is as much an asset as factories and forests. It can be used to market many products other than disposable diapers. For instance, a series of early readers for the kindergarten child – printed, of course, on Kimberly-Clark paper.

PUTTING INFORMATION BACK INTO INFORMATION TECHNOLOGY

This story illustrates an important point. For Kimberly-Clark did not use any sophisticated, state-of-the-art, leading edge technology. They did not let the technocrats take over. They concentrated on the *information*, not the *technology*, and they succeeded.

What was right about the way they exploited the information was their focus on getting the information, recording it accurately, and applying it over and over again. In this case, the technology they chose to use was of little consequence.

Think for a moment about your own company. You are paying hard-earned money to acquire, store and use information. Your employees are being paid to obtain and manage information every day:

- your secretary to record people's names, addresses and telephone numbers
- your accounts department to maintain proper records of sales and marketing expenses
- your salesforce to gain new customers
- your marketing people to keep you informed on what your competition are doing.

The trouble is that this costly information is not managed as if it were an asset. Some of it may be in your head, some in your secretary's filing system, and certainly a great deal of relevant information is somewhere else. It lies scattered and duplicated across multiple local filing systems – some computerised, some not. It is frequently out of date and often contradictory, and is only accessible to exclusive local groups of users.

In developing your Information Asset Management capabilities, three questions need to be answered:

- What strategy should you adopt?

- What system of information management would be appropriate and relevant to you?
- What stages will you go through in developing your capabilities?

Part I of this book addresses the first question, Part II the second and Part III the third.

QUESTIONS

1 Do you have the information you need about your actual and potential customers, particularly their spending habits and propensity to spend?
(a) too much
(b) too little
(c) too late
(d) too approximate
(e) too inaccurate.

2 Do you know why sales are lost or not made?
(a) always
(b) seldom
(c) never.

3 How do you know whether your sales and/or advertising costs are too high?
(a) we keep detailed records and compare ourselves with competitors
(b) we have some information, but don't know about competitors
(c) the agency tells us what to spend.

4 Do you know which of your marketing decisions were right, and which were wrong?

5 Do your systems people spend too much time firefighting instead of providing the information you need?

6 Are top management satisfied with the present contribution from information technology investments?

7

How closely do planned information technology developments relate to the marketing and sales goals of your business?
(a) very strongly related
(b) little relationship
(c) what planned IT developments?

Part I   Strategy

Introduction to Strategy

WHAT STRATEGY SHOULD YOU ADOPT?

To answer this question, I would draw a parallel with the strategies adopted by manufacturing managers when introducing computerisation. In manufacturing, the strategies were:

- the simplification of individual production lines
- the automation of individual production lines
- computer-integrated manufacturing.

In marketing and selling, three computerisation strategies are essential. They interrelate, but conceptually they are very different.

1 *Automation*. The sales and marketing process is accelerated and intensified by *localised automation* of specific information gathering and using functions.
2 *Fusion*. The needs and behaviour of both existing and prospective customers are identified by using one database, formed by *data fusion*: i.e. the collection and merging of data from many different sources.
3 *Integration*. Marketing is made more accountable using a closed-loop planning and monitoring approach based on *fully integrated marketing systems*.

Figure 1.1 shows the main characteristics of these strategies. They are described in outline below, and in more detail in Chapters 2–7.

STRATEGY 1: AUTOMATION

Marketing and sales costs average 15 to 35 per cent of total corporate costs. Much of that results from inefficient use of information. By automating the information intensive functions within sales and marketing, companies have increased revenues anywhere from 10 per cent to more than 30 per cent; reduced costs by 10 to 70 per cent; and achieved investment returns often in excess of 100 per cent. These returns may sound like the proverbial free lunch, but they are real.

Procter & Gamble found that their analysts were spending five hours per day searching market research reports for relevant facts and figures. By automating the retrieval process, they managed to cut the time down to one to two hours daily.

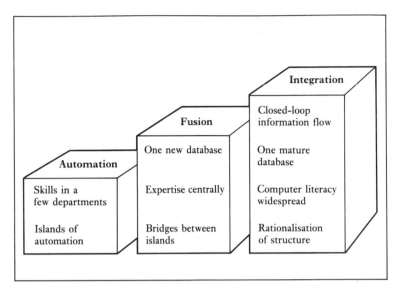

Figure 1.1 The three strategies.

Milton Bradley, the toy manufacturer, equipped their field salesforce with terminals, to help reduce inventory and accelerate orders and shipments. The system sent and received electronic mail; created new orders and checked on outstanding ones; and reviewed sales and shipment activity during the previous six weeks. In consequence, they reduced order entry staff from twenty to three people, and cut administrative expenses by 70 per cent.

STRATEGY 2: FUSION

Is automation a panacea? Definitely not! Automation could make you go out of business faster than ever before. It can make you more efficient in the wrong activities, more effective with the wrong customers, and help you compete better in the wrong markets.

Doing the right thing is more important than simply doing things right. Information about customers can help you do the right thing.

All businesses know things about their customers. This information can be applied to satisfy their future needs. For example, a woman who buys a maternity dress at Sears (US) receives brochures about baby products through the mail some months later.

Casinos try to retain their high-rolling customers by spending as much as 20 per cent of their revenue on complementary services. By amalgamating items of customer data on a computer, Caesar's Palace more accurately identified big spenders, and thus reduced its budget for such services by 20 per cent.

Building a customer profile often requires the fusion of many bits and bytes of data. National Consumer Database, in the UK, takes the largest list of adult consumers available – the electoral register – and overlays the British Investors Database (5.6 million individuals), the Facts of Living Survey (0.7 million individuals) and the Homedata Database (250,000 properties that have changed hands in the last year. Models are then used to 'spread' information. For example, one model estimates the price of every house on the database. While this particular model may not be 100 per cent accurate, there are many targeting jobs for which 95 per cent accuracy will suffice.

STRATEGY 3: INTEGRATION

Automation plus fusion equals integration. This is a 'one plus one equals three' strategy, in which the whole exceeds the sum of the parts.

A good example of integration is provided by a custom printing company which uses a computerised telemarketing system. This provides automation for routine tasks such as the dialling of customers, and the calculation of prices, which speeds up work and helps keep costs low. The system also fuses together data collected by the telemarketers, which enables better and better targeting to be applied to all the subsequent marketing activities, from advertising to product design. As a result of this integrated approach, the company works faster and smarter. The net result has been a 25 per cent increase in sales, which has more than paid for the system within six months.

The idea is slowly taking root that there should be strategies for computerising marketing and sales. Although the systems will take many different forms, the automation, fusion and integration strategies offer useful general guidelines. By the end of this century, these three strategies will have been implemented, and the resulting integrated marketing systems and the associated organisation will generate profitable revenue, enhance customer service and reduce the costs of advertising and selling.

Automation Strategy

Julie Peters, a salesperson for Stevenson Conveyor Systems, was half way through her second cup of coffee when she started her day. She opened her hand-held sales management system and plugged it into the kitchen telephone. The solar powered book computer included a voice and visual module to communicate with customers and people in company. Her action list for that day which appeared on the screen included three sales calls and a number of follow-up items.

Sales Direction Magazine *(January 1990)*

Sales and marketing use masses of information. Automation of information handling is traditionally viewed as a prime objective of any information management system.

Most automation of information management, whether via computers, electronic storage media or telecommunications, is introduced as a rather tactical means of speeding up existing tasks, and consequently saving some costs. It is rarely introduced as a result of a larger picture or strategy. Rather than recklessly attempt to come up with an automation strategy simply on the basis of experience or intuition, the strategic thinker would take a blank sheet of paper and draw up an issue diagram (Figure 2.1). While they seem quite general, such diagrams are useful for thinking through the economic implications of a specific automation proposal. Also, because of their general nature, they can be helpful in identifying alternative options, before committing to a particular strategy.

The major advances of the 1980s – personal computers, word processors, facsimile machines, mobile telephones – have tended to be introduced to support existing methods of working. Still, it is helpful to regard this 'automation of the status quo' as the first, and simplest, of the three strategies for Information Asset Management.

SUCCESS OF AUTOMATION

In many fields, substantial cost savings have resulted from better information management. Few accounting departments in large companies have been unaffected. Tangible savings have been achieved through:

- reducing numbers
- de-skilling work

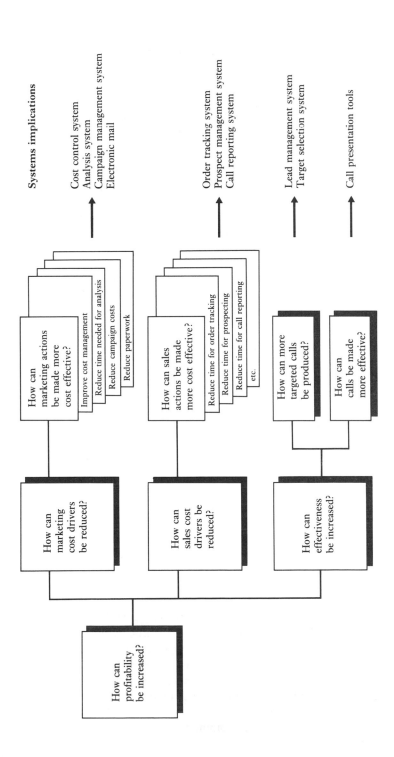

Figure 2.1 The starting-point for automation analysis.

Systems implications

Cost control system
Analysis system
Campaign management system
Electronic mail

Order tracking system
Prospect management system
Call reporting system

Lead management system
Target selection system

Call presentation tools

How can marketing actions be made more cost effective?

Improve cost management
Reduce time needed for analysis
Reduce campaign costs
Reduce paperwork

How can sales actions be made more cost effective?

Reduce time for order tracking
Reduce time for prospecting
Reduce time for call reporting
etc.

How can more targeted calls be produced?

How can calls be made more effective?

How can marketing cost drivers be reduced?

How can sales cost drivers be reduced?

How can effectiveness be increased?

How can profitability be increased?

- reducing overtime
- avoiding hiring outside staff
- absorbing growth within additional staff limits.

Other economies include equipment savings, space economies, improved cash flow and credit control, asset utilisation, stock reductions, scrap reductions, price reductions, and so forth.

Talk about office automation is commonplace. The argument goes as follows: office work consists of unstructured activities, involving text, voice, image and data. New technologies now make it possible to store, process and transmit vast quantities of information in all these modes and to link media in a useful way. Using these capabilities will vastly improve the productivity of staff and management, and will radically change the nature of office work.

The long-term vision is of the office as we know it ceasing to exist, with more and more people working from home or other locations of their choosing. The evidence to date, however, indicates that only the staff functions – especially those of typists – have become measurably more cost effective. The improvements in management productivity are just around the corner, but await the arrival of integration (as described in Chapter 6).

Economies claimed of automation deserve very careful examination. They have frequently been of a theoretical rather than a practical nature and often fail to materialise at all. Nevertheless, evidence of success is mounting. We look now at the related areas of marketing and sales.

HELPING MARKETERS WITH AUTOMATION

What does a marketer do and which marketing functions can be successfully automated?

The terms 'marketing' and 'selling' are sometimes thought to be synonymous. In reality, they describe quite separate activities. Marketing involves analysing the market and devising communications and products to meet its needs. Selling consists of exploiting the opportunities created to produce sales.

The precise role of the marketer depends on the type of product and market involved. For example, a company developing a snack food may use its marketers to define opportunities for new types of snacks, but the product will be designed and developed by food engineers. On the other hand, marketers in financial services companies are often responsible for both the concept and the design of a new product. We examine these differences later.

So what are the common features of marketers' roles? One is the pattern of time utilisation. Several researchers have studied how managers spent their time. Their results are summarised in Table 2.1.

Table 2.1 How managers spend their time

Work activity	Time spent on activity (%)	
	Mintzberg (1973) study	Kurke and Aldrich (1983) study
Scheduled meetings	59	50
Desk work	22	26
Unscheduled meetings	10	12
Telephone	6	8
Other	3	4

Another study by AT&T provided a new insight. It showed that white-collar workers spend 80–95 per cent of their time communicating and managing information!

In principle, tools that facilitate the management of information should make marketers more effective. But what of the tasks they perform, and the computer applications they need to support those tasks?

Studies of marketing management by John M. McCann (1986) show that the work of marketing managers can be broken down into a number of steps, which he summarised as the 'four Ds' of brand management.

1. *Detective.* The brand manager should constantly search for ways in which to improve, which means searching for clues in the market and consumer data.
2. *Designer.* Once an opportunity has been identified, programmes must be designed to capture the opportunity.
3. *Decision influencer.* Brand managers must be able to influence the marketing director and finance director, who often have the final say in decisions.
4. *Diplomat.* The programme is often implemented by others. The essence of marketing implementation in such an environment is the location and removal of bottlenecks obstructing the transformation of a planned activity into an actual product, service or campaign. The brand manager must locate any individuals who are impeding progress. Diplomacy is then needed to remove the obstacles and keep the programme on schedule.

All of these functions can be assisted by automation of information management.

Individual tasks which can be automated, and so made faster, easier and more cost effective, include:

- Researching and analysing the nature of an existing or potential market. Data capture is automated in many ways (which will be discussed further under 'fusion' in Chapter 4). Information retrieval and statistical analyses are often only possible as a result of computerisation.
- Planning campaigns and budgets. PC-based systems with modelling capabilities are used to produce and then compare models of campaigns and budgets. Spreadsheets and decision support tools are widely available to speed up the planning process.
- Designing products, packaging and printed materials. Desktop publishing in-house is increasingly used to reduce the costs, and decrease lead-times of design work.

HOW AUTOMATION MAKES SELLING MORE EFFICIENT AND EFFECTIVE

No business can prosper without selling. Yet it is only in the last few years that industry has started to automate this fundamental activity. These developments have shown that time and information are the key resources of the salesforce. The right systems help make better use of both.

There is plenty of scope to reduce the cost of sales. It is expensive to put a salesperson on the road. The annual cost of recruitment, training, management and other overheads, can easily average out at £100,000 *per salesperson*. Various studies have established that no more than a quarter of the typical salesperson's working time is actually spent with customers.

Even when he or she is about to clinch a deal, the odds against closing a sale are getting longer. Research by McGraw-Hill's *International Management* magazine (1989) into the marketing of industrial products has shown that whereas in 1979 it took an average of four calls to gain an order, in 1989 it took more than six!

And over that ten-year period, the cost of a sale trebled, which takes a nasty bite out of the supplier's margin.

The hidden costs of failing to meet customers' expectations must also be scrutinised. One particularly disturbing research finding is that for every complaint registered with a supplier, there are another 50 that are not, and these result in more than 500 potential customers being warned against the product concerned.

Other research shows the cost of gaining a new customer to be four or five times as high as the cost of selling to an existing one – i.e. a customer in the hand is worth six in the bush.

Clearly there is an urgent need for automation that not only raises salesforce productivity, but also monitors customers' perceptions and reactions. Any dissatisfaction uncovered must be dealt with swiftly and fairly.

In the USA approximately 20 per cent of salespeople use computers in the sales process. A study by Booz, Allen and Hamilton found that IT-aided sales calls could be made 30 per cent or more productive. Another study of users found 71 per cent experienced a gain in productivity and the average gain was 43 per cent (see Table 2.2). While the latter study suffers from self-selection biases, and an unclear definition of productivity, it still indicates the potential advantage of computer-automated selling.

Table 2.2 Productivity gain in companies using salespeople with PCs

Number of salespeople	Percentage reporting gain	Average gain (%)
Under 10	74	35
10–99	68	28
100+	71	45
Average	71	43

Source: *Sales and Marketing Magazine*, May 1987. The survey included 185 companies with a total of 7625 salespeople.

Automation of selling involves simplifying certain tasks and targeting others. Gains come from three areas:

- *Making the right calls*. Much time is wasted making inopportune calls, at the wrong time, and to the wrong person. Time could often be better spent if the right customer and the right time were known.
- *Making each call more effective*. Call preparation and customer presentations can both be improved.
- *Increasing selling time*. Numerous tasks conspire to waste the time of the sales representative, for example:

  - expense reporting
  - unsaleable product returns
  - sample product tracking
  - promotional material distribution
  - call reporting
  - product inquiry handling
  - mail
  - phone tag
  - tickler file management
  - plan-o-grams
  - training
  - incentive/bonus programme
  - dealer publicity tracking

- customer promotion payments
- promotion performance tracking
- order status enquiry
- marketing information collection
- buyer profiles
- call preparation
- customer record updates
- office budgets
- business review preparation
- company car administration
- communication of new product information
- price changes
- personnel administration
- sales analysis
- order tracking
- distribution tracking
- mailing list preparation
- credit problems
- bid preparation
- product recalls
- sales planning
- territory management

The effect of making the right calls is large. For a typical salesforce, 25 per cent of calls produce 75 per cent of the revenue. With a salesforce producing a revenue of £100 million, increasing the targeted calls by 1 per cent would increase revenues by £2.7 million.

The effects of more efficient calls and increased selling time are also large. For sales representatives who make, say, four customer calls daily and produce £100 million revenue, an extra call per week is worth £5 million.

The greatest benefits are to be found with new sales representatives. An information management system helps get the new salesperson up to speed as follows:

- the new salesperson is given a listing of all customers and prospects, prioritised by major customers, regular customers, standard prospects, etc.
- any 'hot leads' are followed and confirmed
- letters go out to all customers and prospects, introducing them to the new salesperson
- the call pattern established by the previous salesperson is followed for the first few months, while the new salesperson settles in
- the new salesperson systematically contacts key customers and prospects to update the 'pipeline' process
- the new salesperson's progress is monitored by management; problems can be identified and dealt with early on.

The productivity of the salesperson improves faster than would be possible without computerising.

The effect can be very dramatic. For example, if salesforce wastage is 25 per cent per annum, and growth 25 per cent, and automation helps the new representative become effective in five months rather than six.

Then with a salesforce of 100 producing £120 million revenue per annum, automation will increase revenues by £5 million.

KEEPING AUTOMATION SIMPLE

Salespeople for the most part simply like to sell. Ask them to learn complex systems with many commands and they will think it a waste of time that will result in unmet quotas. So, forget systems that rely on commands, require more than a nodding acquaintance with a keyboard or have documentation more than one paragraph long.

The consequence of not keeping it simple will be general despondency, plummeting morale, longer lunches and whispers of 'better get my CV out'.

TECHNOLOGY FOR AUTOMATION IN THE 1990s

The 1990s will see new technologies and new uses of existing technologies for marketing and selling. These will bring results as dramatic as those of the last decade.

In the 1980s, innovations such as pocket calculators, portable telephones, word processors, PCs with spreadsheets and fax machines have all raised productivity significantly and become almost indispensable business tools. Their costs dropped as their sales ran into millions.

Office in a briefcase

'Office in a briefcase' facilities will be provided by laptop and pocket computers, linked into the company's computer network by telephone lines and cellular radio. Electronic mail and facsimile services can keep representatives in touch with base even when they are thousands of miles away. Further support comes from personal computers and videotex screens in representatives' own homes.

No longer will salespeople have to spend a high proportion of their working time doing paperwork, travelling to the office and attending briefings.

No longer will they have to put business at risk by delaying the 'close' to take a trip back to the office for price, delivery or technical information. The 'office' will always be with them. This will not only improve call rates, but will enable salespeople to make better use of their own judgement and selling skills.

Information storage

Disk technology is also in for a radical change. Already on PCs we are seeing extra layers of fast cache technology speeding up performance. The advent of erasable optical disks with ten times the capacity of magnetic disks is sure to shake things up, as is the increasing use of CD-ROM.

The user interface — reducing manual effort

There are many ways to interface a computer, in various stages of development.

- The *QWERTY keyboard* has been around for over a hundred years, and we are likely to be using it for a while yet.
- *The mouse* was the big breakthrough in interaction with and control of computer systems in the last decade, and is now an almost indispensable supplement to the keyboard.
- *Optical character recognition* (OCR) can also supplement the keyboard. While OCR has not yet reached the point where it can compete with manual typing, it is improving fast.
- *Voice input* is being developed by the major players, but practical systems for office use may still be several years off. It is actually very difficult to get from a system that can accept carefully spoken English, with a limited vocabulary and a clear separation between words, to one that can accept anything shouted at it.
- *Pressure-sensitive touch-screens* are about to take another step forwards. Touch screens have had a long and chequered history, but the major new development is in screens that can detect how hard you are pressing. IBM have been experimenting with a 'paperlike' interface that can read and interpret numbers, letters and control characters produced with a handheld stylus. They report that this is far more economical then the equivalent keystrokes or mouse clicks.

These interface technologies are of paramount importance. A study by Apple computers has shown that users with WIMP machines use them for 3 hours daily, while non-WIMP users only used them for 30 minutes!

Software environment — reducing the learning curve

What will users see on their screens in the 1990s? How can the software be designed to minimise the learning curve for the millions of future users?

One of the problems of working with a computer for the first time is the conceptualisation of the filing system. Users have to remember where files are placed, and often worry about losing data. By making files visible to users, they have more confidence working with the computer.

As software evolves, it will be possible to go beyond the simple icons used today to add indications of the size and contents of files, let users write notes on the icons, and indicate the age of the file visually.

The user environment will make sure that when icons are moved about on the screen, the appropriate programs are executed. For example, to fax a file to another user, they will pick up the file and drop it onto the fax machine on the screen. The fax software will then ask the user to 'dial' the number or allow quick dialling as on a real fax machine.

Achieving this will not be easy. Packages from different vendors will need to resemble one another. Standards will have to be sorted out. There are bound to be losers – both users and suppliers – just as there were losers when the video standard of VHS rendered BetaMax redundant.

The overall aim of the environment will be to give users confidence, complete functionality and the ability to do most of their work without leaving the screen. Keeping information in the virtual world of the computer will reduce the excessive amount of printing that occurs in the conventional paper-based office. The visual desktop environment must give users the confidence that their information will not be lost or forgotten.

Expert systems — deskilling staff

A product approved in 1990 that presages the future: it is Hewlett Packard's New Wave. Looking superficially like a conventional Windows desktop, it includes a task automation facility known as an 'Agent'. On the screen, the Agent is just an icon, a symbol of a little man wearing dark glasses. A simple Agent task might be to get some monthly figures from a database file, and turn them into a chart.

More complex tasks could involve setting up communications links to get data from a remote data source, putting them into a spreadsheet and presenting the result as a graph. The Agent simplifies tasks by actually doing them for the user. This is a radical departure from just improving the look of the screen.

Another development is the creation of 'hyper' media combining text, graphics, digitised sound and moving images from a video camera, all on the database. Possible business applications are still unclear, but as with all innovations this is something to watch.

Expert systems of a sort have been running on mainframes for decades. Their entree onto PCs in the early 1980s was greeted first with excitement, and subsequently with some disappointment. The reason for this can be found by remembering what an expert system is.

A conventional expert system is really a kind of database, filled with knowledge gained through laborious discussions between the people programming the expert system and human experts knowledgeable in some particular field. Most expert systems are then given some kind of interactive front end, so that the user can get at all this knowledge in a straightforward way, usually by form filling, or having some kind of on-screen conversation with the system.

The problem with expert systems is the time it takes to fill the database with expert knowledge. This has tended to restrict their use to big organisations that have a well-defined problem whose solution can be distributed in quantity to a large number of non-expert users.

Inductive expert systems, and neural networks, are an alternative and very attractive way of programming up an expert system. They dispense with the lengthy process of interviewing, and let the system generate its own rules automatically from a large set of sample data.

For example, a credit risk assessment system could be programmed by selecting a set of credit application forms, together with the subsequent history of payments and defaults. The system might then work out that an 18-year-old male living in rented accommodation was more likely to default than an octogenarian woman in her own accommodation. This information could then be used for automatically deciding credit.

Executive Information Systems – collapsing the mountain of paper

One of the common problems that bedevils most marketing managers is finding time to wade through the mountains of paper landing on their desks. Executive Information Systems (EISs) are destined to meet this great challenge. These systems present key results and performance indicators, tailoring the information to the individual needs of the managers and directors using the system. Senior managers see only summary reports, but these cover wide areas of the business. Middle management have access to deeper levels of detail, but focusing on a narrower business base.

Apart from summarising, time savings are also achieved by exception reporting and graphical techniques. Bad results are shown in red (for stop), middle results in yellow (for caution) and good results in green (for go). Trends are shown with line graphs, comparisons are made using bar charts.

Communications — reducing travel and meeting time

Telecommunications is an area of great potential and one where hard savings have been demonstrated. If your salesforce spend hours sitting in traffic jams, when they could be working, then telecommunications can help:

- pagers provide increasingly detailed messages to the person on the move
- call diversion allows you to divert your calls to a phone in another building – for example, if you want to avoid travelling to the office, you can have calls diverted to your home
- voice mail allows you to store and forward messages and even 'call' a list of contacts.

And the day is not far away when everyone will carry a simple pocket-size communications terminal that can transmit and store both voice and data.

ACHIEVEMENTS OF AUTOMATION

Automation is a necessary phase, and it is the phase that most companies are now in. All the systems building blocks are contained in the automation phase:

- Workstations used by sales and marketing management and staff
- Collection of data into databases
- Data communications technologies
- Use of analysis tools in the planning process.

We learn from automation:

- Which data are important
- Which conflicts and stresses we must resolve
- How to learn and use systems professionally.

QUESTIONS

1	What do you know about the time spent by your sales team: (a) Face to face with clients? (b) Searching for opportunities? (c) Travelling to and from the office? (d) Qualifying poor leads? (e) Digging into paperwork?
2	Does your salesforce maximise face-to-face selling time and make sure every call is an effective call?
3	Can you generally reduce the quantity of paperwork, and the time spent on it, to an absolute minimum for both salespeople and sales management?
4	What do you know about the time spent by your marketing staff: (a) Analysing raw data? (b) Searching for opportunities? (c) Designing possible solutions? (d) Implementing campaigns? (e) Evaluating the campaign's effectiveness?
5	Do you have enough time to identify potential customers?
6	Do your staff and suppliers miss deadlines and delivery times?
7	Do you get warnings of problems before it's too late?

Automation Case Examples

You press the button and we'll do the rest

Kodak advertisement (1888)

This chapter demonstrates different approaches to automation in several industry sectors. The functions of sales and marketing change according to the industry and type of product or market involved.

This is not an exhaustive study, but it will provide insights which will be drawn upon in the rest of the book.

The following industry sectors are examined:

- consumer packaged goods
- consumer durables
- consumer services (including financial services and retailing)
- business supplies
- business plant and equipment

CONSUMER PACKAGED GOODS

Cigarettes, soft drinks, canned and packaged foods, etc., are all produced in this sector. Consumers spend little time choosing these goods, but tend to purchase them frequently, they have some brand loyalty and no after-sales service needs.

Multi-brand manufacturers depend on a wide range for profitability, but often need 'flagship' products to enable the rest to survive. They aim to spread the brand portfolio to cover seasonal peaks and troughs, and need to respond quickly to signs of ill-health in any of their main products.

In many consumer packaged goods companies, these functions are carried out by divisions and regions. One of the great challenges, once automation has been achieved on a local scale, is to fuse together the information and to integrate the systems of the separate areas. The development of corporate technical and data standards will reduce the long-term problems associated with local 'islands of automation'.

Brand marketing is one of the main areas of automation. In the past marketing managers relied upon vast printed volumes of market research tables. It would take them several days, or even weeks, to examine the numbers manually and decide where to pour incentives and where to focus resources. Problems would often go unseen for weeks or months.

Today, brand marketers are beginning to automate their access to, and manipulation of, data. Databases are available with information (internal) extracted from the sales ledger, and salesforce statistics gathered with handheld computers (external), retailer sales and scanner data, competitor sales and activity data from market research, and survey data from market research.

PCs with spreadsheets and gateways to databases are increasingly common. Some companies are using statistical tools. The use of EISs and DSS (Decision Support Systems) has also started to grow significantly. They are still used extensively as *ad hoc* reporting tools. They link into multiple databases, containing sales history, market research, field sales data, etc. While many tools exist, there are few packaged monitoring applications.

The 1990s technologies – advanced workstations with simple user environment, WIMPs and object-oriented programming – are likely to accelerate the penetration of IT into this traditionally high-spending area. However, much analysis and planning is still handled by advertising agencies and market research firms, and many brand managers will resist the computer well into the 1990s.

CASE EXAMPLE – BRAND MARKETING AUTOMATION

Borden is a US branded foods manufacturer that produces dairy, bakery and snack items. One of the time-consuming tasks of the marketing department was to identify accounts or regions that were not performing as well as expected. A sales database containing records of over 100,000 sales with 400 fields can be interrogated using the following automated procedure:

1 Use target reports to assess sales in each region, as per cent of target and per cent change from last year, and shortlist problem regions.
2 Use end-user tools to obtain comparable information for the accounts within the district and shortlist the problem accounts.
3 Use a tracking report to see if the problem lies in the distribution level, or the number of items stocked by the account.
4 Review store audit reports to see if prices are in line with competitive brands in the account.
5 Use the shelf-facings information obtained from store audits to assess whether the shelving matches the requirements of the plan-o-gram agreed by the account.

Steps 1 and 2 identify problem accounts, and Steps 3, 4 and 5 are used to isolate the cause of the problem. The process is highly automated, and the brand manager has time to take actions, rather than drowning in a sea of paper.

Advertising is vital for companies selling low-priced packaged goods, as is merchandising and sales promotion. A 'pull' advertising strategy using TV and mass media is commonest. A very few packaged goods companies have used direct marketing and built customer databases, but this area is growing steadily.

Dialogue with retailers and other channels is handled increasingly through *telephone-order taking*. However, the decision to computerise this function is closely linked to warehousing and distribution decisions, and packaged systems in this area are usually integrated distribution systems.

Field salespeople tend to be of the 'order-taking' variety. Large sales-forces often need their workload to be balanced using territory models. Handheld terminals and laptop computers are used to automate many of the routine order-taking tasks.

CASE EXAMPLE – FIELD SALES AUTOMATION

The field salesforce of Courage sell beers, wines and spirits to independent supermarkets, pubs and off-licences. At any one time, one-third of the products are being promoted, with the dates and times of the promotions varying from customer to customer. The sales representatives take orders and present product and promotion information to customers. The following problems with their working practices led to automation:

- delays of up to three days in the post before orders were received plus a two-day lead time required by the carriers meant that one working week from order-taking to delivery elapsed, resulting in customers' stock-outs and lost sales
- sales staff would often fail to receive promotional information in time because of postal delays, again resulting in lost sales and lost goodwill
- clerical effort for the sales team was considerable
- management information was inadequate and late.

Initial efforts to automate, using videotex, failed due to the inconvenience of using home TV sets for business. A trial using portable terminals was much more successful. These were menu driven and were able to send and receive data electronically.

CASE EXAMPLE – SALES AUTOMATION

A large multinational pharmaceuticals company in the United States has used a voice messaging system to automate communications with its salesforce since 1981. The system is used by over 1000 staff, of whom over 800 are field based. The main justification was that it allowed a consistent message to be delivered quickly to a widely dispersed sales organisation, where time zones left a narrow time window during which communication was socially acceptable. Voice mail was found to be very effective for this function and also had other benefits:

- Significant reductions in sales-related telephone costs were achieved, as well as a reduction in face-to-face meetings
- sales staff could no longer claim that they had not received a message, since the receipt of all messages is logged – this led to a more responsible attitude in all staff
- the informality of the medium has reduced the time spent creating formal memos.

The costs ($300 per user) were considered insignificant when compared with the increase in effectiveness.

CASE EXAMPLE – TERRITORY RATIONALISATION

A company selling a wide range of branded products throughout the UK uses a Territory Rationalisation System to plan territories suited to the needs of their ever-changing sales team. The system shows them where to locate new salespeople for optimum efficiency. Over five years they have re-organised more than 140 times! The steps in this process are as follows.

1 Choose the geography. The most easily accessible common geography is postcode: every address has a postcode, and it is easily discovered. Having such a system enables analysis at a level between looking at individual accounts and merely summarising at territory level.
2 Select the data. You need to base the reorganisation on some hard facts. Who is the salesforce calling on? Is there a recognised balance between regular customers and prospects? What makes two adjacent territories equal in opportunity?
3 Decide on a strategy. Do you build your territories around your salesforce, or do your salespeople have to fit in with your territories?
4 Know your customers. Take the opportunity to ensure that you have a complete record of your current customers.
5 Analyse before reorganising. You will already have an idea of how many territories you need, and what is wrong with your current set-up. However, there is work you must do to ensure that your initial ideas look feasible.
6 Question your coverage. Are you really a national company, or would you just like to be?
7 Use the road network. Never use the motorways merely as territory boundaries – they are not barriers but aids to travel. They should be used as the spines of territories wherever possible.

CONSUMER DURABLES

Electrical appliances, hardware items, furniture, cars, etc., are produced in this sector. These are 'considered' purchases and many questions must be resolved before buyers commit themselves. The buyer needs to talk to the supplier's representative, who will usually be the dealers or retailer in this case. Such products are bought less frequently, and often require after-sales service. Purchases are often made at distinct 'lifestage' times, such as weddings, home purchase, etc.

Brand marketing often plays a much less significant role than with consumer packaged goods. The need for fast access to massive databases showing hundreds of brands in thousands of outlets is less critical. The market often changes much more slowly than for consumer packaged goods.

Sales promotion and merchandising support are given to dealers, and are often the most critical factors to monitor. Databases are available from (internal) sales history and (external) market research.

Direct communications programmes that bypass the dealer, agent or retailer are becoming more common, especially in the motor trade. Sales leads are often generated by the manufacturer and passed on to the dealers, agents or retailers. In this way the manufacturer retains the customer data, and can control the dialogue with the customer.

Field service is often an important aspect of follow-up for electrical durables.

Sales often have a more sophisticated role, and laptop computers are increasingly being used to provide ready access to a wide variety of sales data. Sales management are beginning to use planning models of salesforce size and territory rationalisation.

CASE EXAMPLE – SALES AUTOMATION

The sales support system of Black & Decker (US) helps the 225 people selling 7000 separate items across the United States. The system that it replaced required the customer to mail in the order to a distribution centre, or to give it to the sales representative. Under that arrangement, an order took nearly a week to be entered in the system. With the new system, orders are transmitted by members of the salesforce on their portable terminals at the end of the day on which they are received.

The system offers a popular electronic mail feature. This is used to send price and product announcements from headquarters to the field personnel. Also, the field personnel can query whether a particular order has been shipped or not.

In practice, the representatives tend not to use their portables in front of customers. A rep explains: 'In some cases when I call on a small store, there is no way the owner is going to leave the till and let me use the phone. So I write the orders and transmit them later.'

CONSUMER SERVICES

Retailing, petrol, dry cleaning, bank cheque accounts, credit cards, travel insurance, car servicing, airline travel are all examples of consumer services. The consumer spends a limited time choosing these, and poses a few questions. Convenience of purchasing and using is often the prime consideration.

The branch network is often the most important factor. Planning focuses on geographic opportunities. Monitoring tends to focus on geographic performance, merchandise management and profitability.

CASE EXAMPLE – NETWORK MARKETING AUTOMATION

This US banking group has an extensive branch network, which produced a large volume of data for marketing management. Management introduced a system to give them quick access to the vast amounts of data that used to occupy several hours of their working day. The design of this system provides an optimal ergonomic solution to their needs, automating many of the routine tasks. The system has a number of important features:

- only name and password are needed to access the system – there is no need for any operating system commands
- the workstation instantly receives copies of the core software programs needed to access all facilities
- the 'desktop' is displayed just as it was left at the end of last session, and contains file folders, reports, memos, spreadsheets and graphs
- tools for querying databases or creating spreadsheets are in view
- using the simple point-and-click operations of a mouse speeds up the marketing process – three or four clicks can solve most simple problems, ten or twelve can tackle virtually anything
- most importantly, repetitive processes can be saved up and performed later.

Merchandise planning is important for retailers. It usually has to be integrated with other operational systems, such as purchasing, and cannot easily be developed as a stand-alone automation system. Merchandising problems are often quickly addressed by local cost cutting, in-store promotions, changing facings and listings. Matching the range of products to the local market demographics is important to retailers. Pricing can also be critical, for instance in petroleum retailing. All these tend to require sophisticated integrated data to support them.

Shop layout is also import. Plan-o-grams provide automated tools for shop layout planners. These can be tied into Direct Product Profitability (DPP) methods, to improve store profitability.

Direct marketing is used by many consumer services as a method of increasing store traffic and loyalty (e.g. using frequent shopper promotions), and reaching customers not covered geographically. Financial services and leisure in particular are marketed this way. Customer contact, response handling and follow-up are supported by direct mail and telemarketing systems, although in many cases these are operated by advertising agencies and bureaux, rather than by the retailers themselves.

Field sales are used by high-value services, such as pensions and insurance. Portable terminals and laptop computers are used to automate and improve sales presentations.

CASE EXAMPLE – SALES AUTOMATION

Over 60 per cent of this financial company's employees are directly involved in selling insurance. Most of the business was processed centrally, and time delays of up to five weeks were normal in producing quotations. Portable terminals were introduced to enable the salesforce to produce quotes while actually with the customer, thus cutting out the time delays. This was used for life cover plans, capital insurance plans, life insurance, mortgages with life insurance and pensions.

The cost of development was met by the company, but the salespeople bought their own terminals. The application was launched with an in-house video. The take-up has been over 25 per cent and the results of this have been very encouraging.

BUSINESS SUPPLIES

Such items as paper, pens, small computers, fax machines and thousands of other consumables and small durables come under the heading of business supplies. 'Flagship' products are common and product clutter is a widespread problem. Businesses spend little time choosing, and a high premium is placed on convenience of purchase and price.

Business supplies are most strongly affected by competition, by pricing and by new product development. Suppliers' strategies depend on their ability to reach all those behind the purchasing officers who influence decisions. Sales rather than marketing tends to dominate their thinking. Sales promotion can be important, and both push and pull strategies are used. Market 'stretching' techniques are used to seek out new types of customers and develop products for their needs. Loyalty programmes are also important. The salesforce can have a consultancy role for customers, but this is being superseded by direct marketing methods for many types of customer enquiry. Sales territories are often complex.

Brand management frequently involves resource prioritisation between flagship and other products. Generally this is supported by a few PCs with spreadsheets. More sophisticated analyses are performed by outside agencies.

Market research is important. Usually it is carried out by external agencies, who use Computer Aided Telephone Interviewing (CATI) and statistical analysis tools to automate their work.

For products that have a service element, *field service* systems are becoming common, as are monitoring of dealer performance and customer satisfaction.

Direct marketing and *telemarketing*, both as lead generation and as sales techniques, are commonplace.

CASE EXAMPLE – AUTOMATED TELEMARKETING

DHL recently installed the Brock telemarketing system as part of its sales productivity strategy. After only nine months, they measured a significant increase in performance.

All new business leads were directed to inbound telemarketing, where a cold call can be qualified and the revenue potential assessed. If the potential was less than £5000 the lead would remain with telephone sales; if it exceeded £5000 it would be passed to field sales.

The sales results of leads fed through the telephone sales are assessed by a weekly lead analysis, by a full-time person dedicated to monitoring and analysis. This was the first part of DHL's structured approach.

The second part was account development. A new client is telephoned once a week for a month and fortnightly thereafter. All existing clients who bill between £50 and £200 a month are called fortnightly and those that bill up to £50 are called every two months. This, in combination with new business calls, results in an average of 70–80 outbound calls per telephone representative each day, with an average contact rate of between 28 and 35.

At the touch of a button, the representatives have access to client information, which includes booking and billing information. They can also access information on DHL's services and scripting that helps them respond professionally to difficult questions.

The financial target was to increase the total annual revenue by 25 per cent, but within six months the results were well in excess of this.

Field sales systems using laptop computers are making inroads in the field area. Monitoring of 'sales-in-progress' is essential; service levels also need careful monitoring.

CASE EXAMPLE – SALES AUTOMATION

Hewlett Packard has one of the largest automated salesforces in the world. Each US representative is equipped with a portable computer together with a printer and cellular telephone. The portables all have local applications, such as:

- time management
- lead management
- expenses
- address files
- word processing.

They also have access to the systems that reside in the sales offices and to the national information network, via either the cellular telephone or any other phone. This provides:

- access to information on price and availability of their 10,000 products
- the ability to monitor the status of orders – this is very important, as delays in existing orders can damage future sales
- electronic mail facilities
- access to a software solutions guide, so that if a customer wanted, say, a payroll system that has already run in their industry, the representative could identify suitable solutions through this database.

Today, HP's representatives spend about an hour daily working with their portable computers. A third of the time is on-line to the sales office and two-thirds is stand-alone.

The goal was to increase the amount of time spent with customers and to reduce the amount of non-selling time. Careful time measurements were devised to ensure success. HP discovered that sales representatives spend a little over a quarter of their time in contact with customers. About 15 per cent of their time was spent travelling, 13 per cent in meetings and 31 per cent for sales administration.

Automation resulted in a 27 per cent increase in selling time. This came from reduced travelling time and fewer internal meetings. By providing electronic communications, salespeople no longer had to return to the office to get questions answered. In just 18 months, the order value increased by over $1 billion with no increase in headcount.

BUSINESS PLANT AND EQUIPMENT

Equipment from mainframe computers to earth moving equipment are produced in this sector. Servicing is sometimes also a major profit centre.

Capital costs often make this sector slow to respond to market dynamics. Demand forecasting is frequently carried out three years in advance (although JIT methods are reducing these timescales). Sometimes demand depends on external circumstances – for example, the demand for earth moving equipment may depend on the state of the road-building market.

Brand management usually concentrates on quality improvement and service development. Computers have made little impact beyond spread-sheets.

The sales team are seen by the customer to play a critical role. Pricing negotiation is important.

CASE EXAMPLE – SALES AUTOMATION

Cummins is an American manufacturer of diesel engines and components that markets through a network of distributors and an internal national account salesforce. Although distributors are independent operations, the 750 distributor sales reps maintain a close working relationship and information exchange with Cummins factory personnel. In addition, the 30 national account reps handle negotiations with large customers making major purchases.

Management had several objectives in mind when it established the systems. These included:

- sales productivity
- reaching customers efficiently
- reducing paperwork
- managing information.

Several forms of automation were implemented, including electronic mail and distributor access to information.

In retrospect, Cummins felt that the systems should have been more ambitious, more overdesigned and more integrated. The difficulty of changing or adding features now the existing system is in place is tremendous. However, they continue to refine and add to the scope of their systems, and gradually a plan is emerging of a pool of data that they need. This will take them into the next strategy – fusion. We examine this in detail in the next chapter.

Fusion Strategy

The modern age has a false sense of security because of the great mass of data at its disposal. But the valid criterion of distinction is rather the extent to which man knows how to perform and master the material at his command.

Johann Wolfgang von Goethe

PROFITING FROM DATA

American research shows that the name and other details of every US citizen are processed by computers 40 times every day!

Computerisation has filled the world with data. Yet most data provides a very fragmented picture of the customer. Data would become much more useful if it were interlinked to develop a more complete picture of the individual's wants and needs, attitudes and behaviours.

The secret of the fusion strategy is to join the fragments of this puzzle, to create an electronic image of each individual customer or micromarket.

Unfortunately most businesses fail to capitalise on this database explosion, despite all the improvements in information technology. This is not too surprising. Profiting from data requires a unique combination of power and simplicity. You must be able to:

- draw on data from a wide range of sources
- select the exact data sets you want
- combine and analyse them
- repeat and refine the process until you can see and understand how to profit.

To succeed, you need to pool all the data 'owned' by various parts of the organisation, and make it available to all decision makers, so that they can perform all of these data interpretation tasks themselves. This must be done in minutes, not months.

The satisfaction of these needs, is what data fusion and this chapter are all about.

FUSION STRATEGY OR DATABASE MARKETING?

Why use the word 'fusion'? 'Database' is surely the correct technical term, and will do equally well or better.

'Database', like 'strategic' and 'lifestyle' is just another buzzword in business, and I have to admit that sales and marketing people are as bad as any one else at picking up new words. However, 'database' has to go down as one of *the* most overused and misused words in sales and marketing.

Most direct marketing advertising agencies say they practise 'database' marketing; list people now rent 'databases'; service bureaux are self-styled 'database' processing companies; analysts and consultants offer 'database modelling'; research agencies sell information on 'databases'; printers supply electronic 'databases'. A plethora of relational 'database' software is available for computers, large and small alike.

'Database marketing' means too many things to too many people, so I have chosen to use an alternative term − fusion − defined as above.

'Database marketing' still commonly requires the assembly of a good quality mailing list. Up to the mid–1980s, the gurus of direct marketing preached three factors necessary for effectiveness: List, offer, copy. Today, the word list has been replaced by the term 'database'. However, the thinking has rarely advanced very far beyond this.

What is missing from most existing 'database marketing' systems is management information, e.g. performance statistics, market segment sizes and results, channel effectiveness, survey results, and other types of summary information. The addition of these missing ingredients to the database takes fusion way beyond the realms and capabilities of 'database marketing'.

A fusion strategy signals a new move in the age-old game of knowing the customer, and how to satisfy his or her needs and desires. It solves the problem of 'getting closer to the customer' by creating a databank of information about individual customers, products, campaigns and so forth. This may be taken from orders, sales call reports, direct mail responses, research surveys, etc., and is fused together to build an electronic image of the customer as an individual.

Fusion involves ensuring that every contact with a customer or prospect is used as an opportunity to both update and enhance the information held on the database. Thus a more detailed and informative picture of customers' purchasing patterns and preferences can be developed.

Some marketers may still be inclined to dismiss such concepts as just fancy new names for direct marketing, market research and segmentation. But those with an eye for the future see it as much more than that. The strategist would take a blank sheet of paper and draw an issue diagram (Figure 4.1). This shows that the impact of data fusion goes far beyond the traditional boundaries of direct marketing and even beyond traditional mass marketing.

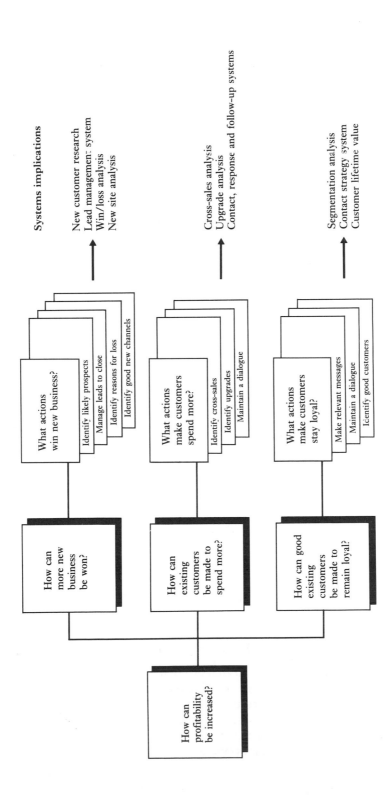

Figure 4.1 The starting-point for fusion analysis.

BEYOND THE TRADITIONAL 'P's OF MARKETING

Fusion strategy represents a radical departure from the traditional mass marketing approach: i.e. concentrating on the 'P's – product, price, place and promotion. Mass marketing has resulted in the 'P's being so conspicuously dominant that the individual consumer has become almost anonymous.

The strength of the small local trader is that he or she knows customers intimately. Special events such as anniversaries and holidays represent opportunities to generate extra sales.

Large businesses have been forced by the scale of their operations to distance themselves from their customers. Market research has traditionally plugged the gap, but it has been no substitute for the hands-on experience and local knowledge of the small trader.

Fusion aims to reinstate the traditional buyer-supplier relationship. Not only will customer information be merged with general market data, but this combination will be personalised before being fed back to sales and marketing.

At present, much of the customer information recorded by companies in the course of day-to-day business lies unused in files dedicated to a specific function. In consequence, computer-based marketing systems do only half the job they could be doing.

Much of the current wastage in sales and marketing can be accounted for by advertising campaigns that should never have been run, or sales calls that should never have been made.

An established customer of a financial services company recently received a personalised mailshot inviting him to subscribe to a new pension plan. There was one flaw in an otherwise immaculate campaign. The customer is in his 68th year – something which could have been calculated quite easily from the birthdate recorded during several earlier transactions.

Data fusion may not be able to work miracles. However, during the next ten years, it will do a great deal to lift information technology out of a supportive role, and make it the vanguard of sales and marketing strategy.

THE NEW DATA FUSION ECONOMY

According to recent research by Hambrecht and Quist, the information-vending business grosses $15 billion in the USA, with growth and profits twice as optimistic as the rest of the American economy. The largest, most profitable and fastest growing area of the information business is marketing information.

Five important forces emerged in the late 1980s which are now forcing businesses to reassess their approach to data fusion and to the customer as an individual:

- 'demassification'
- households
- advertising
- deregulation
- technology.

Alvin Toffler coined the wonderful new word 'demassification' in his book *The Third Wave*, which describes how the mass culture created by the industrial revolution is progressively splintering into the 'demassified' society.

'The mass market has split,' he warned us at the beginning of the 1980s, 'into every multiplying and ever changing sets of *micromarkets* that demand a continually expanding range of options, models, types, sizes, colours, and customisations.' As we move towards 1992, this trend is intensifying. The strategist would draw a market segment cube to examine the dimensions of the problem (Figure 4.2). Along the bottom appear the product categories, up the side go the buyer types, and along the top are the stages in the purchasing process. Each cell in the cube represents a different target for the marketer. The sheer number and variety of these cells is creating major marketing challenges.

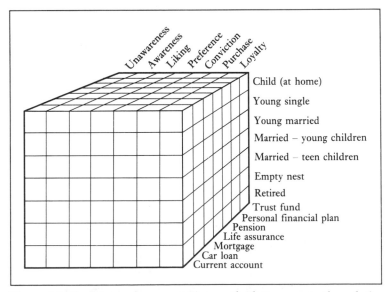

Figure 4.2 Fusion uses segmentation methods to manage the relationship between buyer and supplier.

Revlon makes over 150 different shades of lipstick, more than 40 of them pink. A *Business Week* article pointed out in 1983, 'of the 261 varieties of cigarette for sale today, about half are ten years old or less'. Yet demassification has major problems.

Between 1970 and 1979, 6695 new grocery products were registered in the United States. Only 93, or 1.4%, achieved annual sales of $15 million or more. The cost of introducing a new product has soared. It is said that at least $50 million is needed to establish a national brand in a major category.

Manufacturers and service organisations must keep responding to demassification. To maintain and increase their share of the market in a category, they must demassify their products and services. To understand the needs of the individual, more and more they require data fusion.

And what about the *household*? Remember the good old days when the marketing target was the typical family of husband, wife and 2.4 children? Our 1981 census shattered that image.

Less than 10 per cent of the households in Great Britain fit that description. Half of all households have only one or two members. Single people now head a quarter of all households. The number of single people living alone doubled from the mid–1970s to the mid–1980s. The number of unmarried couples living together tripled in the 1970s. One of the biggest census bombshells was the number of working mothers. To target households, data fusion is needed.

It is not only the market that is fragmenting. So are the advertising media. Ever since television invaded the majority of households, it has been the driving force behind the advertising of consumer products and services. Its power to reach and influence the mass market has been awesome.

Yet the clutter of commercial messages that bombard the average household (some estimate 50,000 messages a year) is causing many viewers who own videocassette recorders to zap past the commercials with the fast-forward control during playback. Mass media are on the decline. Between 1983 and 1988 the ratio of mass to targeted marketing in the United States declined from a 2:1 dominant position to a 1:2 position. The dramatic effect of this change-over on the advertising agencies can be imagined. For targeted advertising, data fusion is essential.

Deregulation made consumer choice the theme of the 1980s. Never before had so many consumers had so many choices: in financial services, travel and telecommunications. In the free-for-all for the consumers' favours, companies jumped feet first into the new world of customer focus. They discovered that it pays to know your customers by name and address and to track each transaction. Before long, they had identified their frequent users, and discovered the benefits of concentrating advertising and sales promotion on the 20 per cent of the market that produces 80 per cent of their revenue. Data fusion is needed to identify this 20 per cent.

The *technology* for a fusion strategy is here. It is providing extraordinary new opportunities to get closer to customers for very little outlay. Computerised details of millions of prospects and customers can be developed, using lifestyle, geographic and demographic information to improve targeting. Special products, services and offers can be tailored to selected segments of databases. They can increase both return on investment and customer satisfaction. The cost of accessing data has fallen so swiftly, and many people don't fully comprehend what computers can offer and can do. In 1973, it cost £5 to access 1000 bits of information (1000 bits equals about 20 words – enough to record a customer's name, address and purchase). Today it costs about a penny to do the same thing.

TECHNOLOGY FOR FUSION

The trouble with all the marketing theories is that, for years, marketers have been struggling with primitive computer tools and, consequently, for every scrap of data. Access to information has been so hard that few have put the theories into practice.

The common complaint is that data processing takes so long making small changes to the data that users never get what they want. One hears horror stories of miniscule additions of data costing tens of thousands of pounds to implement. Data certainly is not yet driving marketing.

Other areas have moved on. They have embraced relational database technology and are reaping the benefits of gaining on-line access to large bodies of data. They can modify the data without having to wait months for DP to effect the modifications. Relational technology is giving users the ability to get at data that is rightfully theirs, and use it in the way they want.

During the past twenty years, a series of Database Management Systems (DBMSs) have evolved, which enable systems developers to relate data items for easier retrieval. This software enables different application programs to share data.

In the early days, 'flat' files with indexing provided advances in programmer productivity. These were replaced in the 1970s and 1980s by hierarchical and network DBMSs, such as IMS, IDMS, TOTAL, System 2000, ADABAS and DATACOM/DB. Although these provided further decreases in programming costs, increased hardware utilisation led to escalating costs, and there was often incompatibility between the databases – multiple databases using different DBMSs could not be linked together.

In 1972, IBM addressed the problem with a ten-year investment in its research project System R. By 1983, the fully fledged relational system DB2 was released.

The word 'relational' has nothing to do with customer relationships (a surprisingly common misconception). A relational database is software that sits between an application program and the data used by the program, and it ensures that the data is well organised and accessible. There are many types of software, but a relational system brings with it flexibility that is absent from most other systems.

DB2 and similar systems (for example, Oracle and Ingres) allow data to be stored efficiently without giving priority to one application and/or limiting the access of all other applications. Data can easily be added and applications extended without the mammoth programming efforts common in the 1970s and early 1980s. The standard language, SQL, allows the sharing of multiple database types.

The primary drawback with relational technology is that, despite the enormous improvements through the years, the hardware is not fast enough to process the largest databases held in relational format. Also, the large investment in existing non-relational systems is holding back many companies. Eventually, with further improvements in software, and with the availability of very large main memories, relational systems will be able to handle ever-increasing volumes of data efficiently.

MANAGING THE DATA: THE CHIEF INFORMATION OFFICER

Most companies are wealthier than they know. Information is a hidden asset which, if managed effectively, can help boost flagging sales performance. Unfortunately it is often not managed at all – data is acquired, stored, distributed, accessed, used and lost at random, and no one has overall control.

The emerging role of the chief information officer (CIO) has been heralded as a solution to this problem. The CIO should be involved with information management in the broadest sense, embracing the gathering, storing, distribution and application of information.

Gathering data requires:

- comprehensive internal and external information collection (not just the recording of successful sales)
- complete information on the markets
- a complete database to create that information.

When storing data:

- one set of corporate semantics must be developed to define the data
- active data and inactive data must be distinguished
- inactive data must be isolated where it will corrupt the resources
- accuracy is vital – only meticulously recorded data, recorded accountably by those responsible, has any meaning. Remember the old adage: garbage in, garbage out.

The CIO should:

- know how to harness the full potential of information
- be an innovative thinker with a global view of business and information needs
- influence the strategic use of information and embed it in the organisation
- bring information systems and people together creatively to solve significant business problems.

QUESTIONS

1 How commonly are you frustrated because different information sources conflict?
(a) never
(b) occasionally
(c) frequently.

2 Do you have trouble pulling together the information that you need from various sources?

3 Are your competitors able to outmanoeuvre you because they have better information on customers and prospects?

4 Where there are inaccuracies in data, whose fault is it?
(a) data processing department
(b) accounting staff
(c) salespeople
(d) marketing management
(e) never know who to blame.

5 How long do inaccuracies take to be corrected?
(a) less than one day
(b) less than one week
(c) too long.

Fusion Case Examples

Nothing is more central to an organisation's effectiveness than the ability to transmit accurate, relevant, understandable information among its members.

Saul Gellerman

As we saw in Chapter 4, the forces underlying a company's adoption of a fusion strategy are more subtle than those underlying automation. The decision to develop a database is based more on strategic insight and business judgement than on the arithmetic of cost reduction that characterises automation. Accordingly, when we look at case studies in this area we shall first review some of the marketing factors that underlie the fusion decision.

The creation of a database does not, of itself, guarantee success. Indeed many companies have built databases, at great cost and inconvenience, which have stood as barely used monuments to technical dexterity; what is usually lacking in these cases is the marketing imagination to create 'applications' of the data: applications are a prerequisite for success. The applications of customer databases include: frequent shopper programmes, clubs, continuity, collectibles, loyalty, lifestage, cross-promotion, line extension, and so forth.

CONSUMER PACKAGED GOODS

The traditional problem of managing the product clutter and maintaining brand loyalty are still with us. They have been joined in the 1990s by several new factors.

Customers no longer accept the marketing philosophy of 'pile it high and sell it cheap' that was characteristic of the 1960s and 1970s. The market is fragmenting and its needs are becoming ever more complex. Lifestyle groups are presenting opportunities to develop new 'tailor-made' products to suit their habits.

Speed of reaction is vital. Consumer scares necessitate overnight changes of plan – benzene in the bottled water, glass in the yoghurt, toxic shock syndrome, pollution, greenhouse effect. Legislation will affect the marketing of alcohol, tobacco and all foodstuffs containing additives.

New direct communication and direct selling methods are emerging for communicating directly with those customers who buy the affected products and for selling 'niche' products. These methods are data driven, requiring the creation of specialist consumer databases.

Information to build databases is available internally from:

- sales history extracted from the sales ledger
- salesforce statistics gathered with handheld computers
- customer data collected from coupons, and 'programmes' involving 'clubs', continuity and collectibles. For example:
  - smokers' database (as advertising tobacco gets tougher)
  - drinkers' database (as alcohol follows suit)
  - mothers' database (product loyalty and line extension)
  - luxury coffee club (product line extension and testing)
  - toy continuity programme (product line extension)

and externally from:

- retailer sales and scanner data
- survey data from market research.

CASE EXAMPLE – CONSUMER DATABASE

Several consumer databases are publicly available, offering the results of fusing together various public data sources:

- the Small Area Statistics of the 1981 census (at enumeration district level – approximately 120 households)
- the electoral roll (about 43 million individuals and 22 million households)
- the Mailing Preference Service (about 250,000 records)
- financial databases (such as share ownership)
- credit data
- house price data
- telephone numbers
- modelling results.

Modelling is widely used to fill gaps or develop clusters. For example, Superprofiles looked at the 4500 census variables and reduced them to 55. Cluster groupings were then constructed to identify 150 discriminators. They were then ranked in order of affluence, using ten derived variables. Finally they were grouped into ten lifestyles:

- affluent minority
- metro singles
- young married suburbia
- country and retiring suburbans
- older suburbia
- aspiring blue and white collars

- multi-ethnic areas
- fading industrial
- council tenants
- the underprivileged.

The whole country can be categorised in this way. Other statistics can then be related back to the clusters.

This type of database offers an easy to understand classification system for the beginner. However, its data is based on large clusters, and there are wide fluctuations between households within each cluster. Experience has shown that, where possible, such data should be superseded by internally derived data.

CASE EXAMPLE – PROSPECT DATABASE

The $10 million Kimberley-Clark 'Huggies' database programme described in the introduction to the book is an example of a prospect database. Each of the three million new mothers added to their database every year is a potential customer. But isn't the $10 million programme prohibitively costly? No, Kimberly-Clark calculated that a family that uses premium quality disposable diapers spends $1300 on them in the first two years of the child's life. By thinking through the arithmetic and focusing on the *lifetime value* of the customer, rather than the *unit sale*, they changed the rules of the entire marketplace.

CASE EXAMPLE – RESEARCH DATABASE

The market research group of Iota, an international soft drinks company, had been purchasing scanner data from a third party for several years. They use this to evaluate:

- promotions
- pricing levels
- deal activities
- new brand introductions.

The research group believed that the scanner data contained errors and ambiguities, and that the data were too massive to be useful. So they introduced a PC to automate routine analysis work and to 'clean' and aggregate the data. Using the PC they can combine market research and sales information to establish quotas, do pipeline analyses, and prepare profit and loss statements. The fusion of different types of data is vital to piece together the complex picture of their marketplace.

CONSUMER DURABLES

Information is available from (internal) sales history and (external) market research. Direct communications are becoming more common, especially in the motor trade. Also, hand-raising programmes and list purchase are being used in direct marketing.

CASE EXAMPLE – PROSPECTS DATABASE

Autohaus Georg von Opel is a German dealer that sells a range of motors, plus service and spare parts. Records of prospects were very poor until the company computerised. A prospect database was built, containing records of every existing and potential customer known to the company. Records are created on the first visit to the showroom, and are only removed if the contact moves house. The system produces a sales activity planner (diary) and is the basis for promotional campaigns. It is also used to track the effectiveness of campaigns.

CONSUMER SERVICES

Consumer service firms are changing from the traditional impersonal product focus to a more personal customer focused approach. Giving customers good service sounds fine in theory, but what is the tough business rationale for being nice?

Take, for example, a supermarket. There are only four ways that a supermarket can use a customer focused approach to do more business. They can:

- attract more new customers
- persuade existing customers to visit more often
- encourage existing customers to spend more
- reduce the number of lapsed customers and losses to competition.

The majority of consumer service firms recognise that customer relationships are the key to their success. Their ambition is to *manage* effectively the relationship between the supply side of their business and the customer. This is an admirable aim, but it is difficult to achieve in practice. It begs many practical questions about individual customers' needs and wants. As mentioned in Chapter 4, the answers to these questions lie in the use of information technology to paint an electronic picture of each customer.

Product profitability databases are becoming common. They are driven by the need to develop profitable products, and to motivate customers to use them. In retailing, many product lines have marginal, or even negative, profitability. In financial services, such products as cheque accounts are unprofitable for the majority of customers. More and more consumer service organisations are developing product profitability databases, merging consumer transaction data with cost data, in order to monitor product profitability. These often fuse together data from widely different sources.

CASE EXAMPLE – AIRLINE PRODUCT PROFITABILITY

The airline business is highly seasonal, and its profitability is very dependent on successful matching of supply and demand. British Airways has developed a database which contains statistics about empty seats on all flights over the past few years. This allows them to develop predictive planning models of future load factors, to help them determine what flights should be available in the coming months. The database uses the DB2 database management system, running on an IBM mainframe.

Consumer data is also being accumulated from internal sources, such as scanners and in-store credit cards, and from external sources, such as geographic databases and market research.

CASE EXAMPLE – FREQUENT SHOPPER DATABASE

In the United States, Frequent Shoppers Advantage Inc. (FSI) are luring promotion-sensitive brand-switching consumers to participate in a frequent shoppers programme. They are using 'smart cards' to make sales promotion a paperless activity. This new development threatens to change the shape of the advertising industry, as well as adding customer focus to retailing.

Coca Cola, Nabisco, Jell-O, Hormel and Frito-Lay are some of the 260 brands participating in the programme, which offers members points that can be redeemed for merchandise.

Consumers are surveyed before participating in the programme. Each customer is issued with a personal smart card. This contains both static information about who the shopper is, and dynamic information about their changing purchase behaviour. The static data includes name and address, credit card numbers, telephone number, and profile information about sex, household, age and family data.

The customer dynamic data includes gross purchases, number of visits, last visit date, average number of items purchased, coupon data, shopping lists, frequent buyer points, buying preferences and other information.

These individual customer databases are the heart of the FSI marketing system. They can be used to determine accurately those customers and prospects who are most likely to buy particular products and services. They can be used to offer customers more or less coupons. They can be used to identify patterns of behaviour that suggest that customers are getting less interested in retail stores and therefore are likely to lapse to the competition.

When customers arrive at the store, they hold up their smart card to be read. The screen springs to life, showing how many frequent buyer points have been earned and the prizes available. It lists the premiums for such items as videotape rental, film development and so on. Special offers and coupons available for card holders are also shown.

In this case example, the coupons offered might be for Huggies disposable nappies. These coupons will have been offered on the basis of the customer's past buying patterns and lifestyle. So, the Huggies nappies coupons are offered to a young mother with a baby, not to non-parents. As we will see later, the number of coupons offered to individual customers can be tailored very precisely to the buyer's needs. Of course this technique does not have 100 per cent accounting accuracy, but it is a significant improvement on older, more wasteful couponing techniques.

The shopper then receives a shopping list. This is printed with items that this individual has bought often in the past. It may also include one or two additional items that are of potential interest. It is printed in the sequence that the customer can most conveniently walk round the supermarket. It also shows items where coupons and specials are available.

At the checkout the shopper again uses the smart card, this time to pay the bill and to see the points collected as a result of the visit. New coupons are shown on the till receipt. This method of delivering coupons is much quicker and more cost effective than any of the traditional methods.

One of the problems that retailers experienced in the past was that after customers had left the store, they were out of reach. Customers who started to go to competitors could not be brought back. However, using this new technology, lapsed customers can be identified by virtue of their lack of recent shopping activity. After a time, a well-written letter can be sent to the shopper offering incentives to revisit the store. Bonus coupons, prize draws and a variety of other marketing methods can all be used to entice lapsed customers back.

Armed with information about who customers are, it is possible to analyse who has received coupons and, if necessary, to work out why they are not working and how to improve performance. For example, a woman with one baby who has not bought Huggies in the past should, perhaps, be offered more coupons. Conversely a parent with many children who already buys Huggies may not need to be given coupons. This type of analysis has been applied widely in the United States to the marketing of products such as Huggies. It has proved enormously profitable for targeting the *right* promotional spend at the *right* consumers.

CASE EXAMPLE – PROSPECT DATABASE

P&O Cruises have a service that carries a large fixed overhead. They tried using discounts to increase level of use, but this failed. They needed to increase the percentage of clients paying full rate.

P&O found they had a hidden asset – a large list of customers who had sailed with them in the last four years. These people were already receiving each new season's cruise programme. It would be too expensive to communicate with all of them regularly, so how could a programme be directed at just the likeliest prospects?

The answer was to get the people to select themselves, by offering free membership of a club that would give them exclusive privileges and benefits. It seemed certain that those who responded would be more receptive to future communications. Accordingly, the POSH Club was developed.

The special privileges for members actually cost very little. They include a bottle of champagne with the capitain's compliments, to welcome them to their cabin, an invitation to an exclusive 'members only' cocktail party, and so forth. The most important benefit is the opportunity to travel on specially nominated POSH Club cruises.

These are attractive cruises that are otherwise difficult to sell. For operational reasons, the two least successful cruises of 1980 had to be repeated in 1981. Both were nominated as POSH Club cruises for that year. Believe it or not they became P&O's most successful cruises of 1981! P&O wrote to just 3000 of their newly nominated members, inviting them to a pre-cruise shore party. They got 800 acceptances! Since then they have run over 16 events annually, and the number of POSH cruises has grown from two to six annually to cope with demand.

BUSINESS SUPPLIES AND SERVICES

Business supply and service firms face many information related issues. Buyers of these supplies and services expect higher levels of personal service than ever before, they do not expect to be treated as faceless customers. Information about buyers has to be collected to understand and fulfil their personal needs.

Information is available internally from orders and enquiries, and can be collected during contacts with customers and prospects. It is also collected externally from dealers and agents, and from research surveys.

CASE EXAMPLE – RESEARCH DATABASE

British Telecom had a deservedly terrible reputation after privatisation. They spent £40 million annually on advertising and customer communications and developed thousands of new products and services. Yet the customers remained baffled as to what they offered, and became more and more annoyed with BT's inability to communicate sensibly. Clearly, BT were wasting their money.

So, they created a database about customers to identify where their communications were wasted, and changed their message to target the individual needs of customers and prospects. The database was custom built, with assistance from consultants, using the IDMS database management system on an IBM mainframe.

BT's particular problem lay in the small business sector. This has always been one of the great challenges to business suppliers – in the late 1970s, Xerox made a strategic blunder in neglecting small businesses, and permanently lost the sector to Canon and other Japanese firms.

BT needed to know who were the different small business targets, and how they should be communicated with. By sending a questionnaire to their customers, they discovered that there is no such thing as the typical small business person, but five distinct types.

- *Enthusiasts*. These people treat telecommunications almost as a hobby, and love to be kept up-to-date with the latest functions and features. All communications with them need to reflect these attitudes.
- *Shopkeepers*. Shopkeepers have very little use for the phone, so there is little justification for communicating with them.
- *Luddites*. They hate everything modern and technical. However, give them a few practical examples, and you might get them interested.
- *Traditionalists*. These people are interested in ease of use and easy maintenance.
- *Corporate executives* – managers and directors of large organisations, trading as small business people. They respond best to arguments about benefits and competitive advantage.

A different communication could be used for each target group. The enthusiasts could be sent catalogues, full of functions and features, followed up by regular updates. They were invited to join the 'Information Exchange'. A dialogue between them and BT developed, sometimes resulting in a sale, but always resulting in a satisfied customer.

Corporate executives, on the other hand, were invited to request a card index of information about benefits and competitive advantage from telecommunications. The customer always guides the dialogue with BT, receiving prompt appropriate information only when requested.

The system is being closely monitored. Programmes that get results are expanded; those that fail are not repeated. By using the database to measure successes and failures, marketing at Telecom is becoming more accountable.

BUSINESS PLANT AND EQUIPMENT

Business plant and equipment firms have similar sales and service challenges to those in business supplies. In addition, the increasing technical complexity of many products has given impetus to developing product databases.

Information is available internally from sales orders, visits, enquiries and from product developers, and externally from economists and industry watchers.

CASE EXAMPLE – CUSTOMER/PRODUCT DATABASE

Menardi-Criswell is one of the top two manufacturers of air pollution control systems. The market, worth $1 billion, is underexploited, with many prospects never contacted.

A database was developed, using outside lists for cold calling, and all enquiries, contacts and customer communications were added to it. Over 6500 active client accounts are recorded. The data is held using the Brock telemarketing software package running on an AT&T minicomputer.

Outside lists have to be 'cleaned' using telemarketing. A call guide running on the Brock system helps the telemarketer gather the required information, and de-skills the job – enabling lower-cost personnel to be deployed.

Contacts are tracked by the system, to ensure that calls are made. Past purchasing history and the relationship with the company are stored, and can be accessed by sales representatives before making a call. Representatives also use their time on the phone to gather demographic information about clients.

Product information, such as pricing, billing and manufacturing schedules, is available on-line for viewing by the representatives. More than 30 form letters are also stored as an integral part of the database.

CASE EXAMPLE – PROSPECT DATABASE

The Shidler Group is a commercial property company in Hawaii. They have thirteen offices across the US. Their problem is finding prospective clients among the ten million businesses of the USA.

Data is collected by 'communicators' based in Honolulu. They pass information to the 13 local offices. This is achieved by a programme of regular calls to real-estate brokers to introduce the Shidler Group, and to encourage brokers to submit properties to their local Shidler Group office for consideration.

For 18 months a manual system was in operation. This involved writing call information on blue cards, then filing them in boxes. As the business grew, this system began to present problems:

- the cards and boxes began to take over the office

- retrieving information became more and more difficult
- many hand-written notes were almost illegible
- management had no overview of the situation.

In response to these problems, a computerised database was developed, using Brock software.

The new system also helps keep the data up to date, by assigning a follow-up date to each record. This electronic 'tickler file' prompts staff to keep in touch with all customers, prospects and intermediaries.

Integration Strategy

It is now technically possible to wire up the nation so that a corporate marketing executive can get instant reports on sales as they happen. And that leads to a fantasy view of the future brand manager, sitting like Captain Kirk on the bridge of the Starship Enterprise, getting reports on sales and then directing the specialists in his marketing crew to pour on instant consumer incentives where competition demands.

New York Times *(20 June 1984)*

FACT OR FICTION?

Perhaps this fantasy contains some elements of the actual future. If so, the marketing manager will be using Computer Integrated Marketing.

Let me use another metaphor. Back in 1920 it took about 15 minutes and the help of a network of telephone operators to call from London to Manchester. The technology was difficult to use, as Figure 6.1 illustrates. Yet by 1960, you could make the same call in seconds, and all by yourself. And just think how easy it is to make a telephone call. You pick up a hand set, punch in a short string of digits on the keypad, and seconds later you and the person you have called are doing business. You can probably even program your phone to dial numbers for you in a couple of dial pushes. No matter who you call, the procedure is always the same. You do not have to worry about the mechanics of telephone switching. All you need is the telephone number.

What happened in the years since 1920 is nothing short of amazing. Simply put, a succession of technological improvements, ranging from dial phones to automated exchanges, turned every telephone user into a telephone operator. To profit from Computer Integrated Marketing, DP departments must effect the same sort of transformation.

Integration is about accessing data just about as easily as using the telephone. It works as follows:

- The diverse sources of information that a company uses is brought together everything from departmental databases to public databases.
- Business professionals are given a single complete set of tools that lets them make strategic use of that data:
  - database query tools and report writers for direct and easy access to data

---
HOW TO PASS AND RECEIVE A TELEPHONE CALL

PASSING A CALL

Before passing a call to the Exchange the subscriber should wait until he hears the telephonist's 'Number, please?' and then, speaking CLEARLY and DISTINCTLY, with the lips **almost touching the mouthpiece,** he should state the number required.

FIRST the name of the Exchange and THEN the number.

The method of pronouncing numbers in Telephone Exchanges has been devised to guard as far as possible against inaccuracies and a description of the system may be of assistance to subscribers.

It is important to remember that the distinctive sounds of consonants become blurred in the transmission of speech by telephone and words containing the same vowels are apt to sound alike. Greater care is therefore necessary in speaking by telephone than is required in ordinary speech, if mistakes are to be avoided.

0 is prounced as 'OH,' with long 'O'.

1	,, ,,	'WUN,' emphasizing the consonant 'N'.
2	,, ,,	'TOO,' emphasizing the consonant 'T' and with long 'OO'.
3	,, ,,	'THR-R-EE,' with slightly rolling 'R' and long 'E'.
4	,, ,,	'FOER,' one syllable with long 'O'.
5	,, ,,	'FIFE,' emphasizing the consonants 'F'.
6	,, ,,	'SIX,' with long 'X'.
7	,, ,,	'SEV-EN,' two syllables.
8	,, ,,	'ATE,' with long 'A' and emphasizing the consonant 'T'.
9	,, ,,	'NINE,' one syllable with long 'I' and emphasizing the consonants 'N'.

ANSWERING A CALL

The call should be answered promptly.

On taking off the receiver, the called subscriber should not say 'Hullo,' or 'Who's there?' but should immediately announce his name.

A householder would say: 'Mr Thomas Brown speaking'.

The maidservant: 'Mr Brown's house'.

Mr Brown, at his office, would say: 'Brown & Co., Mr Thomas Brown speaking'.

His clerk: 'Brown & Co'.

FINISH OF CONVERSATION

The receiver should be replaced immediately the conversation is finished. Subscribers having Private Branch Exchange switchboards should ensure that adequate arrangements are made for **PROMPT DISCONNECTION AT THE SWITCHBOARD.** Neglect to do this may result in serious inconvenience.

Figure 6.1

- spreadsheets to analyse it
- plot tools to view data graphically
- word-processors to add commentary to an analysis.
- The individual tools are integrated seamlessly so that, as users move from one tool to another (e.g. from a query tool to a spreadsheet, for example), the data they are working with can move along with them instantly.
- A non-programmer can quickly build an application that saves a valuable analysis process – such as retrieving information from databases, loading them into a spreadsheet and finally graphing the results – and then automatically repeat the process with just a single push of a button.

- Team members, whether across the hall or across the country, can share electronically not just the final results of their analyses, but also any or all of the individual steps in the process itself – queries, reports, spreadsheets and graphs, even entire applications. So everyone is able to pool ideas, and is working from the same assumptions:
  - brand managers can create the products that reflect research's recommendations
  - manufacturing can prepare for the impact of the sales department's forecasts
  - finance can make sure profit expectations are in line with corporate goals
  - business team members can incorporate any useful techniques developed by colleagues into their own decision making.

When an organisation combines all the capabilities described above into a single integrated system, it can revolutionise the who and how of computer use. Rather than supporting the existing operational functions or automating the status quo, integration supports the strategic functions – planning, execution, monitoring and analysis – that keep a business going.

USING INFORMATION STRATEGICALLY

I hope you now have a sense of how differently things can be done once a business makes the transition to Computer Integrated Marketing. Integration changes the way Data Processing departments meet the information needs of decision makers, and that, in turn, can change the way a company works.

Integration goes beyond the automation of the status quo. Here is what happens:

- *DP departments allow sales and marketing access to data.* This frees DP from responding to routine requests for information, and allows them to concentrate on cultivating information of strategic importance to the company. Since users can get at corporate data, they no longer have to create islands of automation to meet their needs.
- *Sales and marketing make better decisions.* Decision makers and advisers are able to spend most of their time using information, instead of collecting data. Given easier means of interpreting data, they have time to refine their analyses, ask questions differently, change assumptions and look at new data – in short, to uncover ideas and insights previously buried under huge volumes of data.

WHAT SALES AND MARKETING MANAGEMENT REALLY WANT

Over the last five years, I have asked sales and marketing managers in many major companies exactly what they are trying to achieve and what would make them more effective. This is what I have found.

Many companies have a vision: they are moving from mass marketing, based on passive analysis of sales history, to relationship marketing, whereby they forge a long-term relationship with customers, based on a sound understanding of their individual needs and expectations.

This new era of marketing is only made possible by developments in information technology, which allow them to divide their market into closely defined segments. Their advertising and sales efforts are tailored to produce the optimum series of ongoing contacts with each customer. The context, timing and number of contacts is carefully orchestrated on the basis of data about each individual.

Achieving this vision is not an easy task. It depends upon pumping the information round the organisation to satisfy the individual requirements of large numbers of telemarketers, mailing houses, agencies, planners, marketing managers, sales managers, researchers, statisticians, agencies and, not least, the customer. All of these want the right information in the right place at the right time. In effect, the database is the heart of the marketing information system, and the users are the arms, legs, etc.

Integration can overcome four of the greatest headaches of sales and marketing management:

- how to handle the massive volume of data which, by its sheer quantity, wastes management time and distracts rather than focuses management attention
- how to integrate the wide variety of data sources, enquiries, sales visits and orders
- how to co-ordinate the complex data relationships between research, plans, quotas, schedules, forecasts and results
- how to collect and deliver information tailored to individual needs.

Users want to be able easily to switch back and forth between data access and analysis. Once an analysis is complete, word-processing capabilities are needed to make it meaningful to others.

If the process of gathering, analysing and presenting data is worth going through once, it is often worth repeating. Data-reliant sales and marketing managers want a way to save entire data interpretation processes, so that they can be used again to help make better decisions. They are team players. They need to communicate with others in their team. They want to be able to focus on business tasks, not on remembering arcane commands. All the tools must work together in the same way. Data must flow effortlessly from one tool to another, so users do not have continuously to shift gears to perform different tasks.

TECHNOLOGY FOR INTEGRATION

Until recently there has not been a combination of hardware and software that could satisfy all these needs. Just as with the telephone, though, a succession of technical innovations has finally pieced together the solution.

DP departments have traditionally categorised different forms of information systems as

- transaction processing
- office automation
- marketing information systems
- decision support systems
- personal computing.

Originally there was little overlap between these areas. Systems were supplied by different vendors, separately developed and managed, and appeared to serve different users. In fact, these systems have many users in common, and to satisfy them, information is frequently moved manually from one system to another.

Unfortunately, manual interfaces are inefficient and error prone. The secondary users of information, in many cases management, receive outdated or inaccurate information. To overcome this problem, technologists have recognised the convergence of these branches of information systems and begun to integrate them.

The major obstacle to integration has been, until recently, the multitude of vendors, each espousing different standards. However, the standards issue today is becoming less confused, as combinations of industry leaders agree to cooperate, and as a result international standards emerge in the area of PCs, data interchange and communication protocols.

Soon the terms transaction processing, etc., will cease to imply a particular type of hardware or software. Instead, systems will be implemented on a common technical infrastructure, capable of delivering each type of function to a single intelligent workstation. A widely believed view of this infrastructure features a three-level hierarchy:

- Intelligent workstations, like today's powerful PCs, provide the *automation* at the human interface. The advent of powerful and affordable microprocessors has put these within easy reach. Furthermore, well-designed iconic (WIMP) interfaces and object-oriented programming techniques have made it possible for non-technical users to perform tasks previously reserved for programmers, including building their own applications.

- Minicomputers are at the next level, managing local data. Relational database technology and the standardisation around SQL have made it possible to use a single query language to store and retrieve data managed by different database systems.
- Mainframe computers are at the centre, managing the corporate (*fusion*) database and providing broad information collection and distribution services.

The workstations will be connected by a local or wide area network, allowing members of teams around the country (or even between countries) to share one another's work. Systems will be designed with components operating at all levels of the network. Users need not know the location of each particular component on the network in order to operate it.

WHAT ARE INTEGRATED SYSTEMS? COMPONENTS AND STRUCTURE

In a narrow technical sense, a system is a combination of hardware, communications and software (packaged or purpose-built), and on this basis systems can appear quite varied and often confusing. You may be told by your DP (or IT, or IS, or . . .) department that the system is DB2, CICS, MVS, PS/2, OS/2, PM, etc. Yet the technical basis of the system is really its least important feature.

Indeed, a technically beautiful system may be totally impractical. Systems must be built with a view to the *people* who will use them, and with an understanding of how the business in which they work operates. They must deliver the right information to the right people at the right time. Systems must dovetail with people. They must be integrated.

The main *components* of an integrated sales and marketing system seen from a non-technical, managerial perspective, are remarkably constant. These are:

1 *A planning process*. Most marketing systems bear some relation to the classic model of marketing decision making. This starts with the consideration of corporate objectives in the light of the marketing environment [with the usual SWOT (strengths, weaknesses, opportunities, threats) analysis] and concludes with action plans for

implementing particular changes to the marketing mix. This provides the logical framework for the rest of the system.

2 *A set of analytical tools.* These may be used for examining sales and marketing data, to learn from past experience and to evaluate future plans (e.g. what is the best marketing mix?).

3 *A set of physical mechanisms* which carry out the marketing plans. These include the salesforce, other sales channels, advertising, sales promotion, telemarketing, direct mail, customer service and, not least, the products and services. Built into these are ways of channelling information about marketing performance and feeding it into a database, with a minimum of effort or disruption to the people supplying the information.

4 *A database* containing information about customers, their behaviour (e.g. sales) and their reaction to the company's sales and marketing activity (e.g. responses to advertising campaigns); product data; pricing and discounts; advertising and campaign data; sales channel performance; and competitive data.

5 *A control mechanism* for monitoring the data and correcting policy to ensure that outcomes are consistent with plans.

This system, like many, is circular. If we know our customers well, understand them, create the right products and services for them, and remember how well or badly they have received the products and services, we are in better position to serve the customers well next time. In short, the *structure* of the marketing system is a *virtuous circle*. This structure is the main subject of Part II of this book.

Viewed in this way, the systems being introduced into sales and marketing are less of a radical departure than first appearances might suggest. The building of such systems still presents a challenge, however, and the issues need to be understood.

ISSUES WITH INTEGRATION

Integration issues are normally of three types:

- information issues
- customer issues
- organisational issues.

Information issues

Most marketing organisations face the problem of how to integrate the many different types of incoming information. These can include numerical data, textual data, image, voice, and so on. New technologies are currently emerging that are likely to make these types of information more readily accessible and integrated in the future. Hewlett Packard's New Wave product is a good example of successful integration.

Another problem is the temptation to develop rigid databases. In the past this has often been necessary for technical reasons. However, in the future, particularly with relational database technology, it is becoming more possible to develop flexible data structures. *Flexibility* will be vital in the ever-changing marketing arena.

Finally, significant amounts of useful information exist in the public domain, outside a given organisation. One of the challenges facing the information user is how to *obtain* information that exists externally and particularly how to *select* what is useful and important.

Customer issues

At first glance, a consumer might react to a promotion that collects individual purchase information as an invasion of his or her privacy. However, if tangible benefits, such as discounts, promotion redemptions, etc., are received by customers, the exchange of the information is not viewed negatively. The airline industry wrestled with this specific issue in launching frequent traveller programmes. Exchanging privacy, and information, for frequent traveller miles was met with enthusiastic customer response. The definition of *incentives* must be part of the information strategy associated with any new technology for customers.

From a customer's standpoint, ease of use is perhaps a bigger issue. Many technologies have failed in the past because they were difficult for the customer to operate. Ease of use is going to be a Critical Success Factor.

Organisational issues

New technology can disrupt existing organisations tremendously. One of the challenges when introducing marketing technology is to determine what the *existing* organisation can easily do using technology, before ripping apart the organisation to implement a new technology.

Also, users will need significant amounts of training and encouragement in order to assimilate new technologies. Many failures in the past can be accounted for by lack of training.

Finally, the actual focus of the organisation needs to shift from product promotion and the other 'P's of marketing to a customer focus. This refocusing may go further than simple training, and involve internal communication and re-education at a fundamental level.

Although I have raised many issues about the introduction of integrated systems, there are nonetheless many solutions. In fact too many. The secret of success is choosing the right solution for your organisation. This requires a clear vision of where you are going. Part 2 of this book provides one vision.

QUESTIONS

1 How easily can the head of your company get his or her secretary to contact a selected group of customers?
(a) within 24 hours
(b) within 3 days
(c) within 7 days
(d) within 1 month
(e) don't know.

2 Are customer responses being handled with the same high level of professionalism every time?
(a) yes – always 100 per cent perfect
(b) no – often insufficient resources
(c) don't know.

3 Are contacts and responses always followed up at a later date with the same care as personal birthdays and other events?
(a) we are good
(b) we are often slow
(c) some people never get the help they need.

4 How many systems do you need to search to find the information you normally require?
(a) just one system holds everything
(b) two to five systems contain everything
(c) more than five systems
(d) don't know.

5 How well are your technical resources integrated?
(a) all systems interconnect directly, without technical assistance
(b) some technical assistance is needed to interconnect
(c) many systems are technically incompatible
(d) don't know.

Integration Case Example

Last minute doubts led to cancellation of plans for the union of the Nationwide and Woolwich building societies. A few months later, the Yorkshire based Bradford and Bingley and Yorkshire building societies shelved their plans to merge. The difficulty and cost of integrating their respective computing systems was the problem.

Director (June 1990)

There is little experience to draw upon in describing how different industries have adopted integration. Few have achieved it. Therefore, in this chapter I have chosen one concrete example of integration. The subject is sufficiently complex to warrant this detailed treatment.

My description is not of one individual company – for none has fully achieved the sophisticated integration that I shall describe. Rather, I have used real details from several real financial organisations, and combined them to give a realistic picture of a hypothetical company with a very high degree of integration. I shall refer to it as Direct Trust Finance.

The company is a large composite financial services group with a highly respected international reputation. It is also a division of a major bank, and has access to a customer base of over two million people.

Direct Trust saw that the marketplace was being changed irrevocably, and decided to offer 'tied agency' contracts both to the broking community and to building societies.

They wished to attract the right quality of agents in considerable numbers, and recognised that the payment of appropriate levels of commission and provision of tools such as laptop computers would be only two factors in achieving their growth potential. They also learnt the lesson from one of their competitors.

RISKS OF NOT INTEGRATING

This financial service company, Absolute Trust Finance, planned to grow in a similar way to Direct Trust.

They offered laptops to their salesforce, and provided an attractive commission structure. They hired more sales representatives, reorganised territories, promoted the best sales reps to be sales managers and added more products.

However, they implemented this change on an uncoordinated, piecemeal basis.

What happened? As the headcount grew, the unit profits fell. For, with more sales representatives, there was less territory for each rep, less easy pickings, sales reps were younger and less skilled, and management were less motivated to manage.

Next, earnings fell, so the best reps left and the remainder asked for more commission. Eventually, Absolute Trust were priced out of the market,

In addition to avoiding these risks, Direct Trust faces the following marketing challenges.

MARKETING CHALLENGES

The UK market for financial products is changing fast, both in its structure and in the needs and expectations of potential customers. Already economic pressures on profit margins have led specialised financial institutions to diversify into new product areas to get maximum benefit from existing customer bases and to attract new business. There was a time when banks did banking, building societies provided mortgages and people bought life assurance from a door-to-door sales representative. Now we all fight it out together.

Competition will increase further as new companies enter the UK market in anticipation of the Single European Market from 1992. There are over 800 registered companies competing for a share of 25 million potential buyers.

The product is no longer king. In a market where over 1200 unit trusts are on offer, and only 4 per cent of the population are active in the unit trusts, the consumer is king.

The natural order of things is also changing. The average family no longer has 2.4 children, but only 1.8, and family structure itself is breaking up.

Parallel with these developments there has been a very notable shift in consumers' interests in how they handle their money and personal finances. The dramatic expansion in share ownership during the 1980s and widespread media coverage of personal financial matters have contributed to making people better informed on these matters.

The marketing task facing Direct Trust is a challenging one. The market may be expanding but it is increasingly competitive. Selling methods must cater for better-informed customers yet remain cost effective. Customer loyalty must be retained to ensure that opportunities for extra sales are not lost to the competition. All activities must comply with the complex code of legal regulations.

THE INTEGRATED SOLUTION

Direct Trust therefore decided to equip its smaller agents, most of whom had no equipment of their own, with personal computers or laptops, through which an integrated range of technology-backed services could be provided. The specification for this system was as follows (see Figure 7.1 for illustration):

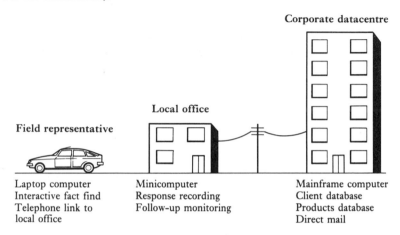

Figure 7.1 **Structure of Direct Trust's systems.**

- A client database, so that agents can target or coordinate their marketing activities. Facilities are provided for agents to download all relevant details from the Direct Trust mainframe computer to their own personal computer before visiting an existing client or a sales lead.
- A database of information on the products available, and historic performance tables across all products and providers.
- An integrated 'back office support system'. This allows Direct Trust to produce sales leads, on behalf of agents, using direct marketing campaigns. The agents pay Direct Trust £10 for each lead provided in this way. (Remember, these details are fact, not fiction.)
- An interactive 'fact find' and 'needs analysis', so that agents can provide financial counselling (covering pensions and retirement planning, lump sum investment, regular savings, life insurance protection and health insurance). This facility reduces the amount of extra knowledge that agents need to acquire in order to be competent. A printed copy of the counselling session is provided for issue to the client.
- The ability to upload from the agent's personal computer to the mainframe, in order to store each counselling session centrally, and to set up effective client and policy records.

To illustrate how Direct Trust and its agents use the facilities, I focus on a campaign to generate demand for one of its products: the personal pension plan.

The secret of Direct Trust's success is that it makes active healthy use of the customer database throughout the integrated marketing cycle. The cycle begins with the use of *research and analysis* to help develop a marketing *plan*, moves on to putting the plan into action through customer *contact*, and then to the *response* and *follow-up*, and *monitoring* stages. The results of this closed loop are fed back into the cycle to be used the next year. I cannot overemphasise the fact that each closed loop stage is dependent upon the others, just as each plan is dependent on those that have preceded it.

DATABASE

The heart of the cycle is the database itself. It is a single database holding detail of all dialogues between Direct Trust and its customers. The database contains information

- who the customers are
- what contacts have been made
- what responses have resulted
- what follow-up action has been taken
- what purchases have resulted.

On its own the database is comprehensive but ineffective. Direct Trust *use* the database throughout the marketing process.

RESEARCH AND ANALYSIS

The first task for the planners is to identify the target audience for the Personal Pension Plan. The database contains details of who has bought the product, but there is insufficient detail to identify the target groups.

A research questionnaire is sent to past purchasers of the personal pension plan. The first group of questions gathers information about employment and attitudes to work. The second group asks about attitudes to saving. The last group covers personal circumstances and demographics.

This research data is gathered using a Computer Aided Telephone Interviewing (CATI) system. The data is then stored on the main database and merged with other known facts about the customers.

Analysis of the data (using Cluster Analysis) reveals three main groups of people:

- *young families*, who have moderately traditional family values and moderate savings.
- *money conscious older people*, with very strong family values and requirements for savings in the pension area.
- *yuppies*, who have low traditional family values and are heavy spenders but poor savers.

PLANNING

Once the target profiles have been identified, the planner then has to locate sufficient numbers of these people to contact.

The mailing list database reveals 20 lists that are possible external sources of the target groups: these will provide 200,000 named individuals.

The internal database contains details of 600,000 people who fit the target profiles – 550,000 existing customers plus 50,000 people who have made enquiries.

The planner also has to decide on the campaign details. Two alternative approaches are available: with and without an offer. The planners decide to use both approaches and to see which is more successful.

CONTACT

Having developed the plan, the next stage is contacting the people. As we saw earlier, more and more use is being made today of direct mail, telemarketing and other addressable media as means of contacting customers.

Direct Trust choose to use direct mail, and adopt the following procedure:

1 The data is selected from the in-house database and merged with data from external sources.
2 Duplicates are removed – although 800,000 raw records are available, after de-duplication, only 550,000 remain.
3 Seed records are added. These allow Direct Trust to police the contacts, by sending sample mailings to the Direct Mail manager's home address. This also helps check security, and unauthorised copying of the mailing lists.
4 The in-house records that have been selected are 'flagged' on the database, to indicate that they have been mailed. The actual numbers from external lists that have been mailed (after de-duplication) are recorded.

5 Output is printed – in this case personalised letters, inviting the recipient to visit an agent – and mailed.

RESPONSES

Once Direct Trust have despatched the letters, responses will start to come in, perhaps through the mail or over the telephone. Sometimes customers will walk into the agent's office. Telemarketing software and agent software will help ensure that maximum value is obtained from every customer response.

Telephone responses should follow a pre-planned routine (often referred to as a script or call guide). The software gives messages and reminders on the screen to help operators guide the dialogue in the desired direction.

After the usual greetings (good morning etc.) name, address and telephone number should be recorded. This will then enable the operator to direct the prospective customer to the nearest dealer. Questions can be answered and information gathered over the telephone so that when the agent and customer eventually meet, each already has details of the other.

At this meeting, the agent, using the personal computer or laptop, is able to conclude the deal.

Finally, if the customer has received an offer in the mailing and wishes to profit from it, they will leave their details with the agent, who transmits them back to Direct Trust's mainframe computer.

FOLLOW-UP

One of the problems that Direct Trust face is remaining in contact with people after they have responded. Prospects who do not buy immediately should be followed up. Using the database, lapsed prospects are identified, by virtue of their lack of purchase activity, and either a letter will be sent offering them incentives to reconsider, or a telephone call will be made. The desired end product of this activity is a sale. Technology plays a very important part in this follow-up targeting.

MONITORING

The huge amount of information involved in the activities of contact, response and follow-up is difficult to manage – there are hundreds of thousands of detailed transactions to monitor. However, the costs of the transactions are high (leads cost £10 each, for example) and it would be foolhardy to ignore what is happening.

Distilling a message from these transactions requires the assistance of a computer. Executive Information Systems (EISs) help. In particular, the new 'traffic light' technology can highlight good and bad areas of the business. Using such technology, the marketing analyst is shown areas where results are good in green (green for go), areas where results are moderate in yellow (yellow for caution) and areas where results are poor in red (red for stop).

In Direct Trust's case, it is using EIS to monitor the effectiveness of its offers.

They may see that the offer produces a higher response rate than the no-offer mailings. However, the response rate is not the most important factor. They may find, for example, that the sales rate is higher with no offer.

This brief tour of the system demonstrates the power of integration. The *same* data was used throughout from planning to monitoring. In a non-integrated environment, gathering and analysing information would take many weeks, sometimes months. Integration automates the process, and makes information available at all stages in the marketing process.

Part II The Virtuous Circle

The Structure

Every declining industry was once a growth industry.
Ted Levitt, 'Marketing Myopia', Harvard Business Review
(July-August 1960)

Just as the early developments in accounting systems highlighted the challenges of putting information to work effectively, so too will the first attempts to do the same in sales and marketing.

Had you asked an accountant in the early days of computerisation what they were doing, you would probably not have received a satisfactory answer. Twenty years ago, the structure and terminology of computerised accounting simply did not exist, outside exclusive specialist circles.

After 20 years of hard work and frustration developing accounting systems, it is now inconceivable that accountants could survive without information systems. We forget how confused everything was at the beginning, and how long it was before a common framework and language emerged.

In sales and marketing departments today, the challenge of capitalising on information is being faced, one way or another. We too need a common framework and language.

ARE SYSTEMS MERELY FASHIONABLE ACCESSORIES?

The primary role of this chapter is to develop a simple, standard framework that you will find useful when considering sales and marketing systems.

However, I have to admit to having a secondary mission too, and that is to clarify the concept of 'systems' in a sales and marketing context. The easiest way to view the term is by looking back through history, where we discover a number of terms that suddenly became fashionable.

'Fashionable' itself was a term that was fashionable for marketers in the 1960s. More recently we have had other buzzwords, such as 'strategic', 'lifestyle' and 'maximarketing'. One of the latest terms to have been picked up again and again in sales and marketing (and it has to be said that sales and marketing people are sometimes buzzword fanatics) is 'systems'.

There is no universal definition of a sales and marketing system. The term seems to be used interchangeably with 'database' and 'information technology' (or IT for short).

There is a vase range of systems available. They differ in:

- *Size.* Some are small, operating on a single microcomputer, some are massive, stretching the capacity of large mainframe computers.
- *Use.* Some are simply databases, some are systems for telephone selling or sales reporting, and some are for market and competitive modelling and forecasting.
- *Importance.* Some are merely 'nice to have', perhaps for dotting the 'i's and crossing the 't's of long-term forecasts. Others are at the core of marketing and sales strategy, perhaps driving the company's whole sales effort or providing new understanding of a brand's customers and their likely response to a new pack size, product feature or promotional campaign.

At this point, the sales or marketing director might feel that because there is no 'standard' system, or because the situation changes so radically every year, there can be no hope of building a durable system. Markets always change, sometimes quickly, rarely slowly. Marketers have to adapt. Some of the changes taking place now are stretching sales and marketing to the limits. Perhaps systems must change too, like any fashion goods?

But sales and marketing create an illusion of change, taking place at an ever increasing rate. If we distance ourselves from the hurly burly of today's marketplace, we notice a high degree of constancy in the needs of sales and marketing.

PRODUCT LIFE CYCLE

The product life cycle (PLC) concept is one of a tiny number of original marketing ideas to enjoy a wide currency. The analogy of product life cycle is founded in the biological sciences and the observation that living organisms pass through an inevitable cycle, starting with conception, passing through gestation, birth, growth, and maturity, and ending in death. This progression is as familiar to us as life itself, and none would deny the inescapable sequence through which the normal organism will pass.

Yet in marketing, the 'macro' product life cycle, showing life and death of products on a grand scale, lacks substantial practical application and relevance. Businesses rarely possess sufficient information about the history of a product group, such as personal computers, detergents or fast food, to make the PLC into the highly specific predictive device that it appears to be. In fact, although PLCs have been used as forecasting tools by a few academics, it is possible to do this only when a large body of information is assembled.

The relevance of the PLC is that it is a constant reminder of the inevitability of change and the stages through which all successful products must pass. These stages and their names are shown in Figure 8.1.

This conventional representation of the PLC must not be taken too literally. For most products, the picture is more complex.

THE MICRO PLC

Figure 8.2 represents a truer picture. Rather than being a slow, smooth process of growth and decline, the profile of a product's fortunes is a rapid, uneven series of events, characterised by growth spurts and sudden shrinkage.

The growth spurts are no accident. They are the product of an activity that occupies most of the waking hours of the real-world marketer – namely the planning, execution and monitoring of *campaigns*. These campaigns may involve mass advertising, direct mail, sales promotion, sales incentives, product adjustment and product development.

Campaigns rely heavily on information for their success:

- analysis and research are needed to establish target markets, attitudes, preferences and so forth
- planning is needed to determine budgets, timescales and the controls that must be put in place during implementation
- monitoring is necessary to detect problems and threats.

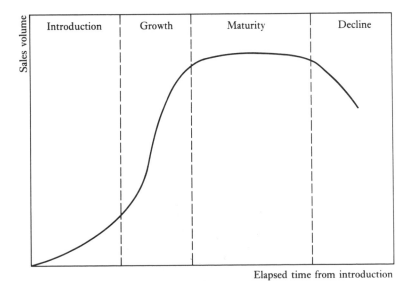

Figure 8.1 Macro product life cycle.

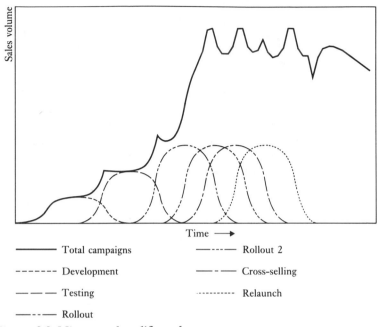

Figure 8.2 **Micro product life cycle.**

The marketer's early warning radar is keenly attuned to indicators of sudden decline, changes of direction, new preferences or new threats. Threats of failure are very real. The US Department of Commerce has estimated that 90 per cent of all new products fail. Faced with this situation, anything that helps to reduce failure rates must be welcome. The obvious place to begin is with a scientific method of observation. The negative factors to look out for vary from industry to industry, but some commonly cited ones, in rank order of importance, are:

- inadequate market analysis
- product defects
- higher costs than anticipated
- poor timing
- competitive reaction
- insufficient marketing effort
- inadequate sales force
- inadequate distribution.

Information has an important role in minimising such problems.

THE VIRTUOUS CIRCLE

In this 'micro-PLC' context, a very simple and appealing picture of systems structure emerges. It involves the closed-loop campaign cycle.

The closed-loop cycle has its origins in traditional management methods. Sales and marketing textbooks refer to 'the Virtuous Circle'. Yet whilst such cyclical methods have been applied with success to the accounting and budgeting functions, they have until recently had limited practical success in marketing and selling as currently practised. However, the advent of modern information technology has brought about the possibility of putting the Virtuous Circle into practice.

As with most business cycles, this one begins with *analysis* and *planning*. Strategies and campaigns are developed by analysing the information available on customer values and perceptions, target markets and old campaigns. Information gathered from in-house data and surveys plays an important role. Computerised tools for summarising and statistically analysing data save time and effort.

Plans are prepared that involve setting budgets, scheduling activities and events, and communicating with those involved. They require a great deal of attention to detail. Databases of cost information assist the budgeting process. Tools such as spreadsheets, desktop publishing and electronic mail help accelerate and intensify the planning process.

When the plan is complete, implementation begins. Customers are *contacted* through what is deemed to be the most appropriate medium: TV, radio, print, telephone or mail. *Responses* from individuals will be stimulated by the initial contact. Often the response methods used will be coupons or telephone. Reaching customers with the right message, at the right time, is crucial. Planned *follow-ups* – by mail, telemarketing or visits – can be prompted by the system.

With all this activity going on, it would be easy for the manager to ignore the details, and consequently lose control. Yet the system can silently *monitor* the details, and only provide reports to management that are timely, relevant and at just the right level of detail to be comprehended during the busy day.

At the end of a campaign, *analysis* of the results highlights any current or developing problems. Lessons from campaigns are isolated and fed back into the next campaign plan. Improved targeting and coordination reduces marketing failures. And so the cycle begins again.

This cycle is illustrated in Figure 8.3.

Viewed in this way, the information systems being introduced into sales and marketing are less of a radical departure than first appearances might suggest.

Figure 8.3 The virtuous circle.

QUESTIONS

1 How is research data disseminated to those who need it?
(a) photocopies are widely circulated
(b) everyone accesses the on-line system
(c) it isn't.

2 What computer tools do you use for planning and budgeting?
(a) spreadsheet
(b) database
(c) decision support system
(d) desktop publishing
(e) pencil and paper.

3 How much of your advertising budget is wasted by duplicated and inappropriate contacts?
(a) less than 5 per cent
(b) less than 10 per cent
(c) less than 50 per cent
(d) haven't a clue.

4 How many of the customer contacts that you make do you record?
(a) over 90 per cent
(b) over 50 per cent
(c) over 25 per cent
(d) less than 25 per cent
(e) none

5 Does top management see copies of or analyse customers' complaints?
(a) frequently
(b) occasionally
(c) rarely or never.

6 A product launch shows signs of being an expensive flop. How would this normally be seen?
(a) a problem to be monitored
(b) a lesson to be learnt from – put it down to experience
(c) something to be forgotten
(d) anybody's problem as long as it's not mine.

Research and Analysis

The researcher's dream come true. Data on thousands of UPCs from thousands of stores 52 times a year. Heaven!
Presentation to US Advertising Research Foundation's 30th Annual
Conference (6 March 1984)

ORIGINS OF MARKET RESEARCH

Marketing might claim to be the world's oldest profession. The buying and selling of products and services certainly has origins that pre-date the Egyptian and Sumerian civilisations.

Scientific marketing, however, involving study of and research into markets, has it roots in the earliest official recording of facts: the Domesday Book, the parish registers under the Tudors, or in the late nineteenth century, and on a more quantitative basis, Mayhew's studies of London's working population.

As Professor Asa Briggs wrote:

by the end of Queen Victoria's reign, very much in English life had been measured. The great official enquiries into environment at the beginning of the reign – in the name of 'the Sanitary idea' – had their counterpart at the end of the reign in the great unofficial enquiries into poverty.

The more specific study of markets and consumer behaviour started in the USA. Towards the end of the nineteenth century, newspapers carried out 'straw votes', which anticipated the development of public opinion polls. This is the time when the term 'market research' first appeared. Charles Coolidge Parlin conducted erudite market studies at the turn of the century and founded the first commercial research company in the 1920s. He even predicted that the USA would eventually have only six or so large motor manufacturers.

There were isolated early developments in Britain, but for the most part the techniques were imported from the USA. From 1920 to 1924 Unilever conducted research among consumers. In 1924 H.G. Lyell founded the first independent research company.

The research industry took off in 1937, when Mass Observation was founded by Tom Harrison and Charles Madge. From their experiences has sprung much of the subsequent commercial research.

The research industry took a leap forward in 1947, when 20 people met informally and decided to form a Market Research Society. The Society took the view that market research consisted exclusively of social, marketing and opinion research conducted in the field among samples of the population. It also ruled that the personal data collected by researchers must be treated confidentially. Collection of data by researchers, for subsequent use in selling or marketing, was outlawed by the Society. This ruling has caused much confusion, and held back the use of individual data gathering until recent times.

Despite the growth of the market research industry, only a minority of businesses have a full-time researcher on their staff. A study by Professor Gordon Willis discovered that only 28 per cent of the companies in his sample had a full time researcher.

THE ROLE OF ADVERTISING

Advertising agencies have been using researchers for more than 20 years. The late Stanley Pollitt introduced a research function, called 'account planning', to keep tuned in to customers and up to date with changes in the marketplace.

Researchers in agencies were seen as 'backroom boys', called in from time to time to produce a few facts, when some clients' problems became pressing. They had no day-to-day input, and although they had closer contact with the consumer than anyone else on the advertising scene, they often had no part in advertising decisions.

Pollitt believed researchers should play a more active role within the agency. He thought they should become planners, who would work continuously with an account, not just at problem times, and should be equal in status to the account handler as part of the account team. It was not until the late 1970s, however, that most agencies had followed J. Walter Thompson and Boase Massimi Pollitt's lead by firmly establishing account planning on the mainline agency scene.

THE INFLUENCE OF DIRECT MARKETING

In the world of marketing of the 1980s, a widespread belief grew up that direct marketers are at the more 'scientific' end of the marketing spectrum. While many of their claims are somewhat exaggerated, they do seem to be beating a path towards a new 'live' market research. Much of their success can be attributed to their modern approach to the computer.

Its influence has been threefold:

- a new set of priorities for market measurements has been introduced – pre-sales promotion and post-sales service have come much more to the fore as subjects for testing and research
- a shift of focus from the product or service to the customer and market segment has meant that customer databases have started to replace or augment the traditional product-based databases
- simple tabular segmentation has been replaced by multivariate models.

TRADITIONALISM IN MARKET RESEARCH

Until the mid–1980s, market research was rather staid in its use of information technology. The advent of the PC and of user-friendly, relatively low-cost software changed this picture dramatically.

The use of IT in market research was, and in some cases still is, limited principally to what is known as 'field and tab'. Questionnaires had to be specially coded and punched by external specialist computer bureaux, and were then analysed on mainframe and minicomputers. While still extremely cost effective for standard, highly quantitative large-scale surveys (consisting of more than 1000 long questionnaires) this approach is being superseded for three reasons:

- The agency and client are traditionally limited to one go at specification and analysis. Much data remains unanalysed. Cost and time limits analysis to the simplest levels – often only hole counts and cross-tabulations. There is little opportunity to explore interesting features that emerge from this first stage.
- The data explosion – the massive growth of virtually free data from in-house computer systems – is rarely taken into account in traditional research methods. The market research industry often regards the data explosion as a threat to its own future – as well it may, if it fails to respond to the opportunities presented.
- The uses of research are changing dramatically. In particular, there has been a shift from 'strategic' research to 'tactical' research. The market is changing too rapidly for the traditionally slow process of data collection, data analysis and data presentation fully to meet the fast-moving needs of brand managers, advertising managers, sales promotion managers, etc. Also 'strategic' generalisations are becoming less and less important, and detailed action-oriented data are becoming more and more vital. As targeted marketing moves ever closer to the ultimate 'market of one person', so the 'facts' produced by the old research are being replaced by 'models'.

THE MOVE IN-HOUSE

Market research companies are booming. At the end of the 1980s the industry was growing faster than virtually ever before, and showing record business figures. However, there is a strong undertow of dissatisfaction among their customers – especially the larger ones, who are beginning to think that agencies are becoming out of date and it might be better to do the job themselves.

Another reason is that many organisations believe they do not have enough control over the research. One company commissioned an agency to find out who its customers were. The agency decided, without consulting the client, to do the research during school hours, when field workers would have their children off their hands. Lo and behold, when the results came in, they showed that only 1 per cent of customers were under 18 – despite the fact that all previous research showed the figure to be 30–40 per cent. The reason? Most young customers shopped during lunch or after school.

Companies need the benefit of research more than ever. The question is whether the market research agencies can meet the challenge. What is not in question, however, is that the computer will be a critically important factor in this debate.

There are two ways in which computers help both agencies and their clients in research:

- data capture, storage and distribution is faster, cheaper and more extensive
- analysis and interpretation are easier, faster, more flexible and require fewer technical skills.

MANAGING RESEARCH DATA

Given the vast quantities of data that do exist, knowing where to begin to collect, store and distribute it presents a real challenge. It helps to differentiate clearly between research on new customers and existing customers.

- For *new markets*, data is comparatively scarce and surveys are often the main sources. Carefully designed analysis methods are necessary to resolve uncertainties introduced by small sample sizes.
- For *existing markets*, fusion can provide a rich information environment. Sophisticated statistical techniques that rely on large sample sizes can be used to provide accurate forecasts and targeting.

Recent developments in the use of electronics, computers and telecommunications for collecting and disseminating marketing data will significantly alter the types of research available to marketing management.

One of the key problems with research is that of data entry. There is often so much data to capture that the process needs expediting. However, while the introduction of hand-held computers would greatly improve the turnaround time of surveys, paper questionnaires remain the favoured method in some markets. According to many market research firms, the investment required to supply several thousand hand-held computers to their mostly part-time interview staff is too large.

Direct entry does have an important role to play in the growing area of telephone surveys. Computer Assisted Telephone Interviewing (CATI) provides interviewers with what is basically a scripted expert system, which enables market researchers to produce very fast results. It has a number of attractive features:

- many software packages are available, some of which cost well under £1000 and run on existing PC equipment
- it increases the accuracy of the information gathered
- it can lead to more sophisticated interviews, where some sort of branching logic is employed
- the analysis can be run off very fast after the last interview
- code frames can be developed 'on the run': that is, when a new brand or item is mentioned to one interviewer, it is automatically presented to the others as a pre-code.

CATI can also be used to gain 'free data' from inbound telemarketing. Most people who call in to enquire about a product or service are willing to answer 10 to 20 questions while talking on the telephone. This produces an excellent source of data, which is useful for learning more about the enquirers, and for developing models to predict their behaviour.

Another way to automate data entry into market surveys is to use optical read-in techniques. Marks showing answers to yes/no questions can be scanned automatically, and Optical Mark Recognition (OMR) can determine the answers with a high degree of accuracy. Optical Character Recognition (OCR) technology still needs to progress a little before it too can be added to the researcher's tool box.

A growing number of supermarket chains have installed scanners, primarily to increase the efficiency of the check-out counters. However, data from the scanners is also fed by the retailers straight into market research analysis on spending patterns and product line movements.

In the USA a number of market research data suppliers, such as Nielsen, TRIM and NabScan, purchase data from these chains for resale to grocery manufacturers. The suppliers operate in one of two ways: they either collect and distribute data from all stores willing to supply them, or they draw a scientific sample of stores in a chain or market. Suppliers who use the second approach present the results at the chain or market levels, but not at store level.

Scanner data are currently being used primarily for testing and analysis. The weekly reporting frequency makes these data much more effective than other research data for spotting promotion/price/product/package changes. The relative quality of scanner data is such that it will almost certainly dominate all other sources as the primary analysis information for retailers and consumer product manufacturers.

Scanner panels are a more sophisticated method. Here, samples of 2000–3000 people in different markets shop in stores equipped with scanners that record data on every item purchased. Most of these have split-cable television facilities that allow the manufacturer to send different or additional advertising messages to a portion of the panel. Scanner panel data will permit the development of different or similar marketing mixes for different demographic segments.

Financial transaction data from card purchases can also yield useful research findings.

CASE EXAMPLE

Barclays Merchant Services has launched Shopper Search, a service based on Barclaycard information which could help small to medium sized retailers target their customers. The service analyses spending patterns created by card usage and can identify which residential areas around a shopping location generate significant volumes of retail sales. About 650 shopping locations and their respective catchment areas are broken into postal sectors containing on average 2250 households. The service gives a Frequency of Visit Report (showing which areas frequently use Barclaycard) and a Relative Spend Report (showing which postal sectors spend more).

ANALYSIS SOFTWARE

The development of PCs that can run sophisticated statistical analyses has had a significant effect on the working practices of marketing analysts and statisticians. As one person put it: 'it means we don't have to go grovelling to the DP manager any more'.

At one time, heavy-duty multivariate analysis could only be performed by a mainframe computer; now it can be done on a PC using inexpensive packaged software. So, the analyst can experiment with all types of techniques, without worrying about the computer cost.

Simple data manipulation can be done using packages such as QPS or SNAP, often alongside spreadsheets and other personal productivity tools. In-house PC-based packages such as MARQUIS and MICRO-TAB are increasingly being used to run smaller surveys with fast turn-around and detailed analysis. Open-ended questions can be grouped, analysed and printed out in the same way as numerical information. Statistical packages such as SAS and SPSS are used by the more demanding statisticians.

CASE EXAMPLE

At a well-known tobacco company, an analyst is investigating what qualities of a cigarette are most attractive to which smokers. He seeks to match subjective impressions, such as flavour or strength, to objective chemical properties. It takes around 40 attributes to define a product. By matching a multi-dimensional matrix of attributes against the sample of smokers, he tries to find an ideal combination in order to produce a cigarette that many people will like. All his analysis is done on a PC using the SAS statistical package.

The trouble is that such computer resources may come to be viewed more as a toy-box than a tool-box. The challenge is to profit from analysis by managing it and directing it to produce useful results. The key to success is for managers to understand what can be done, rather than how to do it.

STATISTICAL TECHNIQUES

The names of statistical techniques are usually excessively polysyllabic, but in essence express quite simple ideas. They can be understood well at an intuitive level. The most popular are:

- factor analysis
- cluster analysis
- discriminant analysis
- regression analysis.

Table 9.1 shows the applications of each of these techniques.

DESCRIPTIVE METHODS

Factor analysis

Factor analysis attempts to find common characteristics of variables, in order to classify customers, products, etc. It summarises a mass of variables into a few key factors.

Table 9.1   Guidelines for the application of statistical techniques

	Factor	Cluster	Discriminant	Regression
Predicts results	No	No	No	Yes
Develops score	No	No	Yes	Yes
Skills needed	High	High	Medium	Medium
Applications	Reduction of question/ answer variables	Segmentation	Segmentation	Segmentation
		Brand preference	Brand preference	
	Merchandise planning	Geo-profiles	Credit scoring	Revenue forecasting

Factor analysis is used to analyse the 400 variables in the census for 130,000 enumeration districts, prior to a predictive analysis. It can be used to analyse customer purchase patterns to find merchandise that tends to be purchased by the same customers.

Factor analysis is extensively employed in the analysis of semantic differential scales. The semantic differential questionnaire consists of a number of pairs of adjectives, on a five (or more) point scale. For example,

Please rate fish fingers on the following qualities:

| Gives good nourishment | □ □ □ □ □ | Gives poor nourishment |

Factor analysis is then used to determine which of the factors in the study is important. By comparison with respondents' ratings of competing products, one may be able to decide what qualities to emphasise in advertising, packaging, etc.

CASE EXAMPLE

A brand leader in the frozen foods market needed to know what criteria affected the crucial area of the mid-week mealtime selection. Consequently they carried out an analysis of attitudes to products designed for this period. Each product was rated for different factors, such as nourishment, satisfying the appetite, etc., so that an overall picture of customers' attitudes to their products was obtained.

Figure 9.1 shows that most of the fish products proved to be popular on the nourishment scale. However, as far as satisfying the appetite was concerned, they rated poorly. The only exception was fish and chips – presumably due to the presence of the chips. The large area of the map unfilled by any existing products presented an opportunity for a product of both a nourishing and satisfying nature.

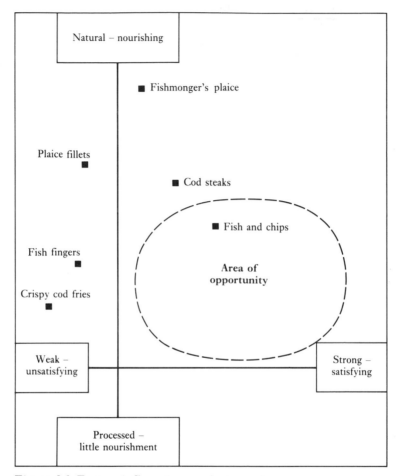

Figure 9.1 Factors influencing product purchase.

The company introduced a product known as 'Cod in Batter', with advertising inviting the purchaser to make their kitchen the best fish and chip shop in town. The result was an extremely successful product with considerable staying power.

Cluster Analysis

Cluster analysis is mainly concerned with the similarity of the objects – their resemblance across a range of variables. It is often used for customer segmentation (see Figure 9.2).

Like factor analysis, cluster analysis is a descriptive technique. It cannot predict levels of response or purchase.

Cluster analysis is one of the main techniques which was used in developing the well-known geodemographic systems (ACORN,

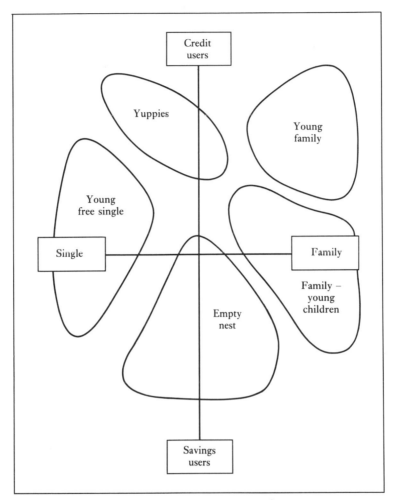

Figure 9.2 Clusters of customers in main market segments.

MOSAIC and PINPOINT). It was used in these cases to reduce the dozens of variables which appear in the 1981 census to a much smaller, simpler set of descriptive variables.

Discriminant analysis

CASE EXAMPLE

A small home-appliance manufacturer wanted to distinguish between innovators (the first 10 per cent to adopt their appliance) and non-innovators. They analysed seven variables connected to a sample of buyers (see Table 9.2).

Table 9.2 Discriminant analysis of innovators and non-innovators

Characteristic	Innovator mean	Non-innovator mean	Discriminant weight
Venturesome	4.88	4.12	3.59
Socially mobile	3.93	3.20	3.08
Privileged	3.68	3.25	2.04
Social integrator	4.13	3.78	2.44
Status concern	2.00	1.73	0.95
Interest range	5.27	5.00	0.59
Cosmopolitan	2.77	3.03	(2.86)

They used this to calculate a score for innovators and non-innovators (see Table 9.3).

Table 9.3 Classification of innovators and non-innovators using discriminant score

Point score (range)	Innovators (%)	Non-innovators (%)	
57.6–60.0	1.7	—	
55.1–57.5	5.0	—	
52.6–55.0	8.4	—	
50.1–52.5	11.7	7.5	
47.6–50.0	18.3	5.0	
45.1–47.5	23.3	20.0	
42.6–45.0	18.3	17.5	
40.1–42.5	10.0	7.5	
			cut-off
37.6–40.0	0.0	20.0	
35.1–37.5	3.3	7.5	
32.6–35.0	—	7.5	
30.1–32.5	—	5.0	
27.6–30.0	—	0.0	
25.1–27.5	—	2.5	

Using the scoring formula developed with a small sample of customers, the appliance manufacturer can categorise all prospective customers as innovators or non-innovators. As a result, it has stopped wasting money by advertising to non-innovators, and through better targeting of innovators has greatly improved the cost effectiveness of its campaigns.

Regression analysis

Regression finds its main use in tackling the problem of predicting behaviour based on people's characteristic profiles. You can use regression on a sample of people of known behaviour, and create a model linking their behaviour to their characteristics.

CASE EXAMPLE

An American insurance agency solved major performance problems using multiple regression. In the early 1980s they produced 750,000 qualified sales leads annually in response to over 15 million mailings. In the mid–1980s they faced dwindling response rates from the ten million small businesses who made up its market. During the late 1980s it used multivariate regression to cut through the fog to achieve better response rates.

Most of its customers were in 'open-collar' industries – people who work with their hands, such as electricians or restaurant owners.

First, they carried out a univariate analysis of their historical responses, looking in great detail at who was buying.

Petrol station owners were profitable prospects, returning $1446 per 1000 pieces mailed (18 per cent above the all-occupations average). On the other hand, consultants had a high response rate as sales leads, but substantially underperformed on all other measures, returning only $554 of premium per 1000 pieces mailed (55 per cent below average).

Geography was another useful univariate measure. Oregon is an excellent state for lead generation (with 2.6 per cent response), but overall it only produced $940 in premiums per 1000 pieces mailed (23 per cent below average). In North Carolina, on the other hand, sales conversions were so strong that despite only average performance on lead generation (1.5 per cent response), it produced $2080 of premium per 1000 pieces (70 per cent above average).

These seem easy rules to apply. Perhaps Oregon and consultants should both be avoided? The problem is that this simplistic approach shrinks the market dramatically, leaving the bulk of the market on the cutting room floor.

The solution is to ask *multivariate* questions. Are petrol station owners (normally good) in Oregon (normally bad) better than consultants (normally bad) in North Carolina (normally good). These questions cannot be answered with elementary statistics. But these are precisely the kinds of problems that multiple regression analysis powerfully and quickly solves. Those factors that are of no consequence are discarded. The important factors then form the basis for a model.

As a test of the power of modelling, the insurance agency segmented a mailing into 13 cells according to score value. The high-scoring records dramatically outperformed the low-scoring records.

QUESTIONS

1
Is market research in your company
(a) allocated a formal budget?
(b) updated regularly?
(c) rarely used?

2
How well do you know your competitors' strengths
and weaknesses?
(a) better than they know themselves
(b) pretty well
(c) moderately well
(d) hardly at all
(e) not even sure who they are.

3
How closely are sales, production and advertising
activity tied to research data?
(a) completely
(b) partially
(c) hardly at all.

4
How are your main brands regarded?
(a) better than the competition's
(b) equal to the competition's
(c) less well than the competition's
(d) don't know

5
How is research data presented?
(a) large printed volumes of tabulated data
(b) on-line computer system
(c) don't use research data.

Planning

Vice-President: *You may take my desk, my secretary, and my phone, but you may not take my computer.*
Professor: *What do you do with the computer that makes it so valuable?*
Vice-President: *I use it to think!*

Bruce McCann The Marketing Workbench

The notion that a computer can be used by planners as a mind expander and an assistant in creative work is comparatively new. Interest in these broader uses of computers flows from recent successes in integrating narrow computer applications to make a broader, more integrated, whole.

What planning tasks can be supported? Strangely, little is known about marketing and sales planning, and there are not many books specifically about this area. Since planning is often associated with sales and marketing, that hardly seems to do it justice. So, before we look at the computerisation of planning we need to look at planning itself.

THE PERILS OF NOT PLANNING

'If you make a better mousetrap the world will beat a path to your door.' This piece of homespun philosophy, attributed to Ralph Waldo Emerson, has characterised the approach of thousands of business failures. Many have been failures due to lack of market information to support their plans.

CASE EXAMPLE

From 1928 the Animal Trap Company of America produced millions of five-cent mousetraps. However, its president, Mr Chester M. Woolworth heeded the old saying, and regretted it ever since.

The company seemingly went about planning sensibly. The new trap had a streamlined appearance and was moulded in black plastic. It had a hole just the right size for the mouse to go in, and when it nibbled on the bait, it would be dispatched by a spring mechanism. The new trap was extensively tested, and never missed. It was modern, it was effective – it was also a colossal flop.

Why was it such a failure? Subsequent research showed that when a mouse is caught using a conventional trap, it is disposed of by throwing it into the garbage *without removing it from the trap*, to avoid the unpleasantness of handling the dead creature. The new trap quite simply *looked* too expensive to throw away!

Mr Woolworth then produced the eminently quotable counter-saying: 'Fortunately Mr Emerson made his living as a philosopher, not as a company president'. The two sayings should be on a plaque by the desk of every would-be marketing planner.

LEARNING TO LOVE THE PLANNING TASK

Planning has long been thought of as a central part of the job of sales and marketing. During the 1980s, the inadequacy of old methods of planning was gradually recognised. This led to the recruitment of many specialist planners (increasingly the career path for the MBA graduate).

As far as possible, strategic marketing planners distance themselves from the image that the public has of marketing – hype, buzz, inspiration and (a little) alcohol. While agencies may cry '*eureka*', planners rely on careful campaign design, give careful briefings, allow plenty of time for execution and understand exactly what is to be achieved and how to achieve it. Sales targets and quotas are set scientifically. When campaigns are launched, there is no rush. When the campaign is in the field, all resulting enquiries are handled professionally and swiftly, optimising customer satisfaction. When the campaign is over, results are analysed to identify what worked best.

Or so we would like to believe. This picture is a dream, but it is one that is slowly being translated into reality. For many, the 1970s and early 1980s was the age of inspiration. We are entering an age of professionalism – an era of management skills and attention to detail.

Most companies are trying to be more methodical about the planning and execution of their sales and marketing – both long- and short-term. This applies in every discipline: brand and product management, pricing, advertising and sales promotion, field sales, branch sales and sales management.

They are beginning to realise that the relationship between expenditure and return in marketing depends as much on the professionalism of management in planning costs and resources as on the innovativeness of strategy.

While there is no perfection anywhere in management, it is still disappointing for companies to find out how weak their marketing strategy is, and how messy their planning and implementation compared with the textbook ideal. Worse, their performance is much poorer than that of their colleagues in other departments. Many strategic sales and marketing plans are often no more than simplistic financial budgeting, or grandiose and often unrealistic statements of aspirations. And making plans 'more sophisticated' misses the point.

The consequences of poor planning are identifiable in terms of late responses to opportunities and competitive challenges, spiralling sales costs, lost market share and high advertising costs to achieve a given effect.

Yet from the viewpoint of sales and marketing managers, strategies may be seen as 'window dressing', plans as obstacles to running the business, and planning as a drain on valuable time and resources. In short, many sales and marketing managers detest planning. Part of the problem stems from the lack of automation of the planning task itself.

Experience suggests that two essential requirements of an effective strategy are simplicity and clarity. Particularly important is an overview.

A clutter of detailed information exists throughout most companies, and this jams up the planning process.

What is needed is a clear, simple, consistent framework that everyone involved in planning accepts and follows – information systems have a vital role to play in developing this.

EXAMPLE – CAMPAIGN PLANNING

Take the planning of campaigns, for example. Some marketers now use a campaign planning system, which supports the following functions.

1 *Reviewing opportunities/history*: the system provides a view of past campaigns, so that whether selecting resources for the next campaign, or simply looking for ideas, answers are available to those critical 'what happened?', 'what opportunities?' and 'what if?' questions.
2 *Recording the campaign*: next, the system helps create and maintain, in a structured manner, the important details of marketing activities. Marketing campaigns are at the highest level. A marketing campaign might be to sell credit cards to the current bank customer base during the period January to April.
3 *Recording the contract strategies*, which are a specified series of contacts received by a particular target audience in the course of a campaign. For example, a series of three mailings to consumers over 35 years old.
4 *Defining the treatments*, which are individual activities, associated with a date, audience, product group and message. In the above campaign, one treatment may be defined as a 20 January mail drop of the 'Gold Card' brochure to the top 10 per cent of the over–35s.

Any variation of these three characteristics would be defined as a separate treatment.

PLANNING TEMPLATES

Marketing plans begin with customers, markets and products, and then determine the promotion, pricing, distribution and service policies. They are usually prepared on an annual basis, and carry with them a budget for executing the marketing programme for the entire year. They usually are rolled up from detailed plans, arranged hierarchically. For example:

- corporate marketing plan
- product group plan (or strategic business unit or sector)
- brand plan or product plan
- product line plan.

The format and contents of the detailed plans need to be defined so that the consolidated plan can be readily produced, and so that budget requests can be judged on a consistent basis.

Templates are becoming increasingly common as a mechanism for ensuring consistency. They are standard forms that are issued to all those responsible for producing a part of the plan. Templates are readily computerised using PCs. Spreadsheets such as Lotus 1–2–3 or Excel are used to produce quantitative plans. Use of cell protection helps ensure that users cannot easily damage the spreadsheet structure. Word-processors too can be used to construct outlines of plans. The planning steps are typically as follows:

1 Corporate marketing (CM) prepares the templates. A planning group meets to ensure that all parties will be able to use the templates.
2 Copies of the templates are prepared for all those individuals responsible for preparing parts of the plan.
3 Templates are distributed to these individuals. They fill in the gaps in the template with their preliminary plans, and check for accuracy.
4 Individuals send their preliminary plans back to CM. They check them for reasonableness.
5 CM communicate with individual planners to resolve any problems with the preliminary plans.
6 CM prepare an overview, showing a consolidated picture of individual preliminary plans. Preliminary budgets are allocated.
7 CM communicate the preliminary budget allocation to individual planners. There follows a round of discussion and negotiation, in which the preliminary allocations are changed. Individual planners

need to know quickly the impact of budget cuts (or rarely increases) on their planned results. 'What if' analysis plays an important part here.

8 CM finalise the budget allocation.
9 Individual planners adjust their preliminary plans.

This sequence is summarised in Figure 10.1.

All these planning tasks can be made more effective by the intelligent use of computer technology.

The computer tools available to assist the marketing planner take a variety of forms. All the following can be implemented using currently available technology. A possible configuration for such a system is shown in Figure 10.2.

- *Personal computers* provide the planner with information storage and processing capabilities, without having to go cap in hand to the DP department.
- *Local area networks* are used to link together the personal computers on the same floor, or even throughout the same building.
- *Word-processing* and *desktop publishing* are used to prepare high-

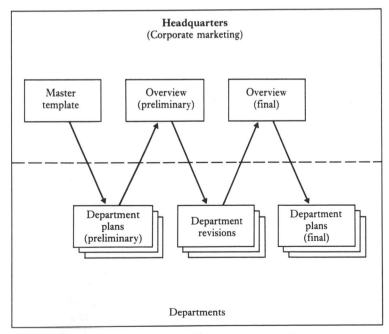

Figure 10.1 Planning templates help ensure consistency and speed of review across different departments.

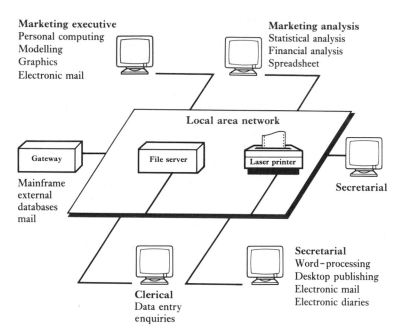

Figure 10.2 A management information system.

quality documents. They are used to type, edit and prepare documents combining text, data and graphics.

- *Spreadsheets* help to speed up the calculation and recalculation of figures, in columns and in tables (e.g. for monthly plans for one to three years). They become essential when budgeting, since they greatly speed up the impact analysis calculations.
- *Electronic mail* systems transmit messages, documents and data quickly and easily between individuals at different locations.
- *Databases* support the rapid retrieval of management information. These may be stored at another location, in which case there is a need for a 'gateway'.
- *English-like query tools* enable the planner to carry out *ad hoc* analyses, without needing to consult the DP department.
- *Windows* allow the planner to bring together several pieces of information onto one screen, and to cut and paste information from several sources on the screen onto one workspace (e.g. a spreadsheet).
- *Gateways* provide access to external databases. These may require some tools that are able to access multiple databases (e.g. FOCUS or SAS). They may also involve the use of a modem to communicate with remote locations.

QUESTIONS

1 What level of planning do marketing and sales make?
(a) high – we cover all eventualities
(b) moderate – we plan some things but others are done by the seat of our pants
(c) low – we make an outline plan and change it to fit the circumstances as they happen.

2 Do this year's plans take account of last year's successes and failures?
(a) reasons for missing or exceeding last year's targets
(b) reasons for campaign failures and product launch flops
(c) reasons for increasing or decreasing sales performance
(d) none of the above.

3 Do this year's budgets take account of last year's success and failure rates?
(a) response rates
(b) sales conversion rates
(c) productivity trends
(d) cost over-runs.

4 Do your plans show how you will acquire new business?
(a) from advertising responses
(b) from cold calling
(c) from referrals by existing clients
(d) other sources of business.

5 Do you calculate accurately the number of new prospects each sales rep needs to find to achieve his or her new business target, and take actions to make it happen?

6 Do you delegate to your salespeople the task of producing accurate, detailed sales forecasts for every customer and known prospect, therefore achieving total advance commitment?

7 Can you set up a new or relief salesperson with immediate full effectiveness?

8 Are you able to rapidly restructure sales territories for maximum effectiveness with minimum demotivation?

Contact

Money comes slowly and by sacrifice. Few people have enough. The average person is constantly choosing between one way to spend and another. Appeal for money in a lightsome way and you will never get it.
Claude Hopkins, author of Scientific Advertising *(1923)*

A sale is one of the most personal of all transactions. It involves thinking, feeling, imagination and trust, as well as an exchange of money for goods and services.

Before exploring the specific techniques of getting more sales, take a moment here to review the elements that make a sale satisfactory for both buyer and seller. Each satisfactory sale should include:

- *An agreement.* This is the simplest and most visible level of sale, yet the most often abused. Your part of the agreement is to provide products or services of at least equal value to the money that the buyer gives you in exchange. Success at this level means ensuring that what you sell provides value for money, while improving, simplifying, beautifying or otherwise adding something to the buyer's business or personal life. This makes the buyer happy and leads to trust.
- *Trust.* All sales agreements should be based on trust and respect between buyer and seller. If a sale is appropriate to your customer's wants, needs and ability to pay, that sale will lead to satisfaction and build trust. Remember the British Telecom case study – BT identified the needs of enthusiasts and Luddites, and built trust with each according to their different needs. Any sales that are not built on trust will hinder the development of an interdependent relationship.
- *An interdependent relationship.* A good sale should be the beginning of a long-term relationship. Remember the Huggies case study – mothers went back to buy more and more Huggies, and spent $1300 during their two-year relationship with Kimberly-Clark.

The best way to sell a product or service is to locate a need in the marketplace that you can fill, and then fit your product or service to that need. Identifying needs is not an abstract or passive process. You and your staff must remain sensitive to how the customer expresses real or perceived needs during the course of a sales transaction. The desire to respect buyers' values is the hallmark of the good seller.

THE COMPUTER-AIDED DIALOGUE

Most customers need time to choose. Studies of selling indicate that sometimes buyers need as many as six contacts with the seller before they are ready to buy. The development of a dialogue with the buyer is therefore an important part of successful selling. Gone are the days when a monologue was effective.

The trouble with a dialogue is that it takes time – and time is money. For instance, it can cost £200 to put a sales representative in front of a prospective customer. It simply is not cost effective to use face-to-face contacts indiscriminately throughout one's dialogue with customers.

The right kind of advertising can help, and it is no coincidence that many advertisements today invite the audience to respond; so beginning the dialogue.

Gathering and disseminating information is essential when helping buyers to choose your product. You must ask questions such as 'When do you intend to buy?', 'When will you next need assistance?', 'What other products might interest you?'

A computerised system can help to organise this information. Responses should be recorded on a computer so that the system can analyse them and trigger the right follow-up activity. If, for instance, the follow-up involves a sales call, then the system should help the sales representative arrange the call, and provide the information needed to be most helpful to the buyer during the call.

Information systems can help sustain a dialogue with customers, moving them towards purchase and ensuring they remain satisfied after the purchase, and that they purchase additional or replacement products later on. Without a dialogue system, there tends to be a one-way flow of junk advertising, 80 per cent of which is wasted.

CASE EXAMPLE

Dylakor of California sells IBM compatible computer equipment, mainly to major Fortune 500 companies. Typically there are many people in each prospective client company who may be interested in buying from Dylakor. The buying process can involve a dialogue with up to 20 people over a two-year period.

A dialogue is initiated when Dylakor writes to a company which is a known IBM site. This is identified from computerised lists of IBM sites. As responses to the letters come in, each person's interest is recorded on a computer. As the dialogue progresses, these details may need to be accessed by:

- literature fulfilment
- sales office
- sales representative
- contracts department
- shipping
- accounts receivable.

CASE EXAMPLE

Information is a key ingredient in the selling process for this company selling business services to Times 1000 companies. Buyers normally invite proposals, and through a series of stages business is won or lost. A study of the issues causing them problems throughout the selling process is illustrated in Table 11.1. Many of these issues can be avoided or overcome through the gathering and recording of information systematically throughout the selling process, and through a win/loss analysis of successful and unsuccessful bids.

USING CONTACTS EFFECTIVELY

The first step in the dialogue is to find the right person to contact. As we have seen, advertising can help by inviting people who are interested in your product to identify themselves. The expensive contact methods, such as sales visits, should be used sparingly for the top customers. Less expensive methods, such as telemarketing and direct mail, should be used for less valuable but more numerous customers. As Figure 11.1

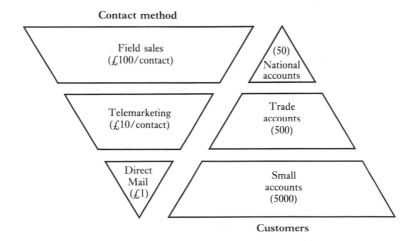

Figure 11.1 Pareto's principle applies when matching the contact method to the customers.

Table 11.1 Key issues

Performance factor	Buyer issue	Seller issue
More bid lists	Don't know product	Don't target communications Don't use right media Don't know market needs
	Don't like response to bidding process	Don't handle bids effectively Don't properly understand bidding process
	Don't have enough friends and allies	Don't recruit enough friends and allies Don't offer right incentives to decision influencers
Less fallout	Don't like presentations	Don't have enough sales professionalism Don't have right pre-sales support
	Don't respond to needs	Don't understand needs Don't care about needs
	Don't act competitively	Don't respond to competitive situations Don't identify competitive situations (until too late)
More wins	Don't like product features	Don't understand winning features Don't offer winning features
	Don't have enough friends and allies	Don't maintain relationship with friends and allies
Less cancellation	Don't like implementation	Don't manage relationship during implementation. Don't maintain implementation quality.
	Don't find product reliable	Don't trouble-shoot problems.

shows, this is an application of Pareto's principle, with 80 per cent of the contact costs going to 20 per cent of the customers.

In today's fragmented marketplace, the role of mass advertising must change. Instead of influencing everybody, a proper role for advertising is to attract, interest, sift out, identify, gather together and communicate with the comparatively few people who are the immediate prospects for what is being advertised.

With the information systems available to sales and marketing management in the 1990s, this is becoming more of a practical proposition than ever before.

On the one hand, we have the technology-driven expansion and fragmentation of mass-market media. Cable and satellite TV, for instance, will lead to 60 new channels in the next few years. Desktop publishing is dramatically reducing the cost of entering the advertising industry; it is also fuelling a move in-house.

On the other hand, database technology is having the opposite effect. The 'fusion' strategy, described in Chapter 4, is resulting not in audience fragmentation but in audience aggregation. With computer-driven printers and enclosing machines, customers and prospects can now be reached *as individuals* in their millions.

Consequently, we are faced with a new problem. More than ever before, we have to communicate precisely if we are to avoid the communications traffic jam.

THE COMMUNICATIONS TRAFFIC JAM

Don't you love direct mail? Probably like me, you see it every morning, forming a small mountain under the letter box.

Dear Ms Shore,

You have been personally selected by our computer to win a special prize . . .

Information technology is presenting a threat as well as an opportunity. In the wrong hands, computers are very adept at targeting the wrong people or transmitting the wrong message. And research shows that most consumers perceive the need to take in more information about products and services, while keenly feeling that they have a reduced amount of time in which to do so. I believe that one of the success stories of the 1990s will be the progress that will be made in getting the right message to the right people at the right time.

It was not so long ago that Acorn was the only name that marketers associated with targeting. Already we have the growth of second and third generation targeting systems. Many marketers are doing ingenious work on segmenting and profiling their customer files. Telemarketers are developing better means of cross-selling and up-selling to an existing customer base. Sales leads are being generated and distributed to sales representatives' laptop computers.

Having come so far, the question must now be asked: 'What is the lesson to be learned about achieving effective targeting?'

CHOOSING AND SCHEDULING YOUR MEDIA MIX COST EFFECTIVELY

An advertising campaign has four development phases:

- *Strategic formulation*. The advertising need is determined and objectives defined. Target markets are specified and media alternatives are identified. This task is normally part of, or an adjunct to, the product planning or business planning process.
- *Media selection*. Particular media to be used in the campaigns are chosen. Normally this associates a medium with a target market and a message to be carried to that market.
- *Campaign development*. The copy, artwork, audio and visual materials, etc., are generated and disseminated.
- *Result tracking*. Enquiries and sales are analysed to assess the effectiveness of media and for tuning the present campaign.

As with all complex projects, this flow can be managed and supported through computer technology. The extent of computer use depends on the company. Often, smaller companies will use agencies' computer systems to help them.

During strategic formulation, a database of the key parameters of the campaign should be recorded.

During media selection, systems are available to show key parameters of the media. These systems reflect the differences in how advertising media are sold.

- Magazine advertising, particularly the trade press, has a typically long lead time between submission and printing. Many software packages for magazine advertising support the entry of editorial calendar information.
- Newspaper advertising has a shorter lead time and is mass-market oriented, meaning that placement decisions are critical. Systems can support careful analysis of circulation data and readership demographics.
- Broadcast advertising (TV, radio) is a numbers game, controlled by ratings and viewer/listener demographics. Audience analysis is the overriding concern of broadcast media management programmes.
- Direct mail and telemarketing offer much more specific targeting opportunities. List brokers offer systems showing the detailed breakdown of their names and addresses.

TARGET MARKET — MASS MEDIA REACH

How can the advertiser contact the maximum number of potential customers? Which newspapers or magazines have the highest readership penetration of the right sort of buyer? How can the best use be made of the advertising budget? These are the sorts of questions constantly faced by any marketing manager responsible for drawing up a media schedule.

Support is currently available from the database research agencies. For example, by comparing a geodemographic profile of the target market with the profiles of the publications in the *National Readership Survey*, opportunities can be quantified. Media titles can be ranked according to readership penetration, the number of potential customers, or even the cost per customer reached. As an example, consider how to advertise for skiing holidays (see Table 11.2).

Table 11.2 Advertised skiing holidays

Readership penetration		Potential customers ('000s)	
Times	128	*News of the World*	303
Sunday Times	127	*Sun*	255
Daily Telegraph	126	*Sunday Mirror*	213
Sunday Mirror	90	*Sunday Times*	126
News of the World	89	*Daily Telegraph*	90
Sun	87	*Times*	37

In terms of readership penetration, the quality end of the market scores highest. However, ranking by numbers of potential customers shows a very different picture. The message should read 'head for the *Sun* if you want snow'.

Similar types of applications for mailing lists are available from the main list brokers.

REACH AND FREQUENCY

Reach may be defined as the unduplicated proportion of a population that is exposed to the advertising message at least once during the designated time period (usually four weeks). *Frequency* refers to number of times within the period that a prospect is exposed to the message. Frequency may be expressed in two ways: average or distribution. If frequency is expressed as an average of 3.0, for example, the average prospect is exposed to the message three times during the period. But certainly not all prospects are exposed three times: some people may be exposed five or six times during the period, while others may not receive the message at all.

Table 11.3   The distribution of contact frequency

Number of exposures in period	Number of people exposed
1	25
2	20
3	45
4	25
5	15
6	5

So it may be important to determine which market segments should be exposed and how frequently. It is clear that different people are naturally exposed to different degrees. For example, people in social group A/B will be exposed to adverts in *The Times* more than people in social group D/E.

The danger is that companies will simply waste an increasing amount of money by enthusiastically promoting to the top groups, instead of refining their targeting to make sure that their advertising is targeted at prospects with real potential.

FREQUENCY AND COORDINATION

A common problem for companies who have different product groups all running campaigns at the same time is to ensure that certain target segments are not overcontacted. For example, a cosmetics company selling 20 perfumes, 10 lipsticks, etc., is likely to find most of its product managers want to contact social groups A/B and C1 just before Christmas.

Campaign coordination is a solution to this problem. Marketing groups meet to identify areas of potential cooperation or of possible overlap or conflict. They coordinate their broad intentions, and priorities are agreed for the coming year.

Templates such as those described in Chapter 10 are useful tools for coordination, and linked into a computerised 'marketing workbench' the task of campaign coordination can be speeded up and made more powerful.

TARGETING AND FREQUENCY

Having established target segments, say by regression analysis, the planner's aim should be to focus the high-frequency (and high-cost) contacts on the high-potential segments. For example, the frequency distribution shown in Table 11.4 was selected by a major automobile company for its direct mail campaign.

Table 11.4   Frequency distribution

Frequency	Score range	Database (%)	Sales rate (%)
5+ times	>0.090	10	8.0
3 times	0.061–0.089	10	3.0
2 times	0.041–0.060	20	2.4
1 time	0.028–0.040	30	1.8
No contact	0.000–0.027	30	0.8

In this instance, the planners determined the contact frequency on a *break-even* basis. In other words, contacting the second decile (score 0.061–0.089) will generate a contribution that precisely pays for three mailings.

Once again, such calculations are most readily done using spreadsheet software.

PROMOTION BUDGET

There are many different strategies that a marketer can adopt, within given budget constraints. Spreadsheets are useful tools to help allocate budgets. Two generic strategies are *push* and *pull*. Push involves aiming promotional efforts at channel members such as retailers, wholesalers, dealers and other intermediaries, rather than consumers. Pull involves attempting to create consumer demand. The type of strategy is reflected through the media plan. Possible allocations of £2 million are shown in Table 11.5.

At the tactical level of the media plan, Table 11.6 shows the publications selected within the press media.

All these types of calculations are greatly assisted by the use of spreadsheets and planning templates. Also, the flow-through of data from the 'reach' databases to spreadsheets will greatly facilitate budget impact calculations.

Table 11.5 Possible push and pull allocations of a £2 million promotion budget

Media	Push	Pull
Consumer media	£120,000	£1,370,000
Trade media	£160,000	£20,000
Personal selling	£900,000	£400,000
Consumer sales promotion	£20,000	£200,000
Trade sales promotion	£800,000	£10,000

Table 11.6 Possible expenditure within the press media

Media	Push	Pull
Good Housekeeping	£30,000	£400,000
Family Circle	£40,000	£500,000
She	£50,000	£470,000
The Grocer	£90,000	£12,000
Supermarketing	£70,000	£8,000

QUESTIONS

1 Do you know how much you can afford to spend to get one more customer?
(a) we have a formula – it depends on the customer
(b) we always spend too little, our views are very short-term.

2 Do planned dates and audiences for advertisements ever conflict with other activities?
(a) other promotional programmes
(b) other activities of sales staff
(c) staff holidays
(d) other holidays.

3 Do you contact the right people, with the right message, at the right time?

4 Has your company ever been embarrassed by cold contacting the wrong people?
(a) royalty
(b) deceased
(c) moved away
(d) competitor.

5 How much of your advertising budget is wasted by duplicated and inappropriate contacts?
(a) less than 5 per cent
(b) less than 10 per cent
(c) less than 50 per cent
(d) haven't a clue.

6 How many of the customer contacts that you make do you record?
(a) over 90 per cent
(b) over 50 per cent
(c) over 25 per cent
(d) less than 25 per cent
(e) none.

7 Do you choose media as a result of reviewing a history of its past effectiveness?

8 Do you have enough time to identify market opportunities and assess their magnitude?

Responses

Two weeks ago, the New York Times *magazine carried an ad for an off-the-shoulder black-and-white formal that some women readers thought they might die for. One of them, this reporter, naively assumed the dress could be bought, and set out to buy it.*

The first stop was Bloomingdale's in the Short Hills Mall in New Jersey. Although the sales help there breathlessly admired the picture of the dress, they said they didn't have it. Nor did the B. Altman & Co. or Abraham and Strauss department stores there.

The next day, this now suspicious reporter went to Macy's at Herald Square. The saleswoman was not amused. 'If one more person shows me that picture . . .' she said peevishly. 'We don't have it, never had it and aren't going to get it,' she continued very, very calmly.

Wall Street Journal *(10 May 1985)*

Finally, when the reporter confirmed that the dress was not available, she called the manufacturer (Lesley Fay) and asked what was the point of the advertisement. She was told it was not really a product, but showed the type of products that Lesley Fay makes.

There is unrelenting critical acclaim, in the trade press, for the latest flights of fancy in advertising, but whether the advertising was successful in leading people to respond is hardly ever mentioned.

As companies grow, responsibilities are split up and handed out. The managing director is busy running the company and managing its assets. The marketing director is busy allocating and approving advertising budgets and developing that breakthrough new product. Product managers are busy building up their advertising recall scores and getting their dealers to stock up and provide a good display. The sales promotion manager is busy distributing money-off coupons, making deals with retailers and promoting novelties from Hong Kong as prizes. But – or so it would seem – nobody is busy worrying about the responses that the advertising is creating.

THE VALUE OF RESPONSES

The Lincoln Mercury automobile provides a good example of the value of responses. Advertisements for the Lincoln Mercury contained an 0800 number so that interested people could respond for more information.

A large number of responses were generated, and 25 per cent of them turned into buyers. Over $300 million in sales were attributable to this response mechanism.

A study of responses by Inquiry Systems and Analysis indicated:

- 60 per cent of all responses purchase within a year
- 60 per cent of your respondents are also responding to your competitors
- 50 per cent of new business is directly linked to a response.

In studies that I have conducted in the computer industry, the figures are nearer to 90 per cent. Responses to campaigns in this area often cost as much as £50 to handle.

In the insurance industry, a vivid illustration is provided by Australian Mutual Provident. Their insurance sales representatives pay Aus $12 from their own pockets for responses generated by the company's advertising.

In a recent survey, business customers put contact with a capable inside salesperson at the top of a list of their wants and needs (see Table 12.1).

Table 12.1 What business customers want most

	Ranking			
	1970	1980	1985	1990
Contact with outside salesperson	1	3	5	5
Frequency and speed of delivery	2	1	1	2
Price	3	2	3	4
Range of products	4	5	4	3
Contact with capable inside salesperson	5	4	2	1

Source: Andersen Consulting.

THE VALUE OF COMPLAINTS

One particular type of response is very important but often neglected – the complaint.

Complaints are an inevitable part of business life, however good your product or service. You must offer the customer a convenient, quick and effective method to register complaints.

The value of registering complaints was demonstrated in an American study, known as TARP, carried out in the late 1970s. This surveyed customers' attitudes before and after complaining.

The hidden dangers of poor and indifferent customer service were shown by looking at registered and unregistered complaints. For every complaint registered, by letter or telephone, there were 50 complaints unregistered. Each unregistered complainant warned an average of 11 friends and acquaintances. In other words, 550 people were discouraged, for every complaint registered.

The value of resolving complaints was also demonstrated. Where the complaint was registered, but not resolved in the customer's favour, the customer was twice as likely as a person with no complaints to remain a loyal long-term customer. Where the complaint is resolved in the customer's favour, the ratio increases to six times, and where resolved quickly, to nine times.

RESPONSE TRACKING AND TELEMARKETING SYSTEMS

Response tracking is an integral part of telemarketing, and is normally offered as part of a telemarketing system. There are more than 50 such packages to choose from: some of the leading ones are Brock, Edge and TelAthena.

Successful response tracking marries technology with meticulous planning and follow-up. It is a process for:

- recording and fulfilling enquiries
- setting appointments
- qualifying leads
- membership renewal
- order taking
- cross-selling or up-selling.

Response management is the process which links contacts to follow up, as shown in Figure 12.1.

The information that is captured, from initial responses received and subsequent sales conversions, can help advertising and marketing management measure the effectiveness of their advertising. In addition, response tracking systems provide the salesforce with a valuable database that permits them to establish a dialogue with interested prospects and develop both prospect and customer profiles.

Any company that is spending money generating responses needs some sort of response tracking system. Responses must be managed effectively, and followed up quickly to ensure that interest is still warm. Slow follow-up will cause complaints and result in lost opportunities.

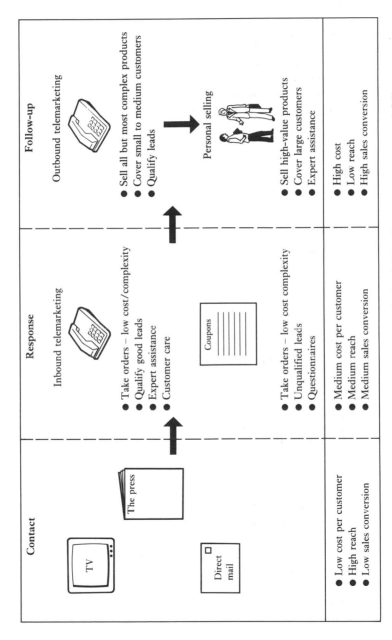

Figure 12.1 Response management systems provide the bridge between contacts and follow-up.

TYPES OF SYSTEMS

A manual system – the old shoebox type – is still used and can be effective, as long as volumes are small. However, an organisation with a large salesforce, a nationwide dealer network or large territories to cover, will usually require something a little more sophisticated.

The coupon-to-database system is common amongst fast moving consumer goods (FMCG) manufacturers, who pass coupons for redemption to an agency or bureau. A database is then created, as part of the mailing process. This valuable by-product can then be used for follow-up.

In a one-way system, a response is recorded and the request is fulfilled. Responses are then distributed for follow-up, to the field or the dealers. No feedback is received about the effectiveness of the subsequent follow-up activities.

In a closed-loop system, feedback on the subsequent follow-up activity is recorded by the salesforce or dealers.

RESPONSE QUALIFICATION AND SCORING

All responses are not of equal value (see Figure 12.2). Free offers frequently attract a large number of 'offer junkies', and literature is widely collected by universities, polytechnics, libraries and their corporate equivalents. Following all responses with equal energy would be a great misdirection of resources.

The trouble is, which are the good responses and which are the bad? While sometimes the title or address can provide a clue, it is usually necessary, deliberately and systematically, to gather the information needed to separate the wheat from the chaff.

What information helps? Although there is no standard formula that can be applied across all industries and products, a call to any company selling facsimile machines, for example, will provide some ideas. In most cases you will be asked:

- How soon do you intend to purchase?
- Do you have a budget?
- What is your job title?
- Have you bought our product before?

These and similar questions quickly provide the sales reps with the clues they need to assess your value. They then filter out the responses into several groups, such as:

1 no awareness of product or service
2 awareness of company

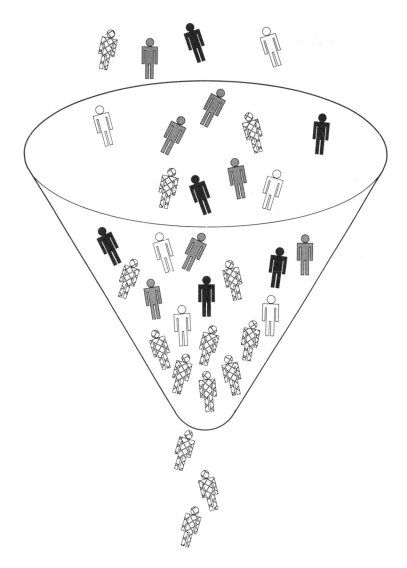

Figure 12.2 Responses are not all of equal value.

3 awareness of product or service
4 positive perception
5 recognition of personal benefits
6 objections overcome
7 ready to buy.

The dialogue will move the customer up this 'ladder'. By recording details of every response, we know where the respondent is on the ladder, and can vary the communication accordingly.

Sometimes the answers to questions do not readily allow you to decide how close the person is to buying. A scoring formula can help here. Each question is given a weight, and each response is scored according to that weight. See Table 12.2 for an example of how this might work.

Table 12.2 Scoring potential buyers' responses

Question	Weight	Answer	Score
Wants a product within:			
1 month	10	Yes	10
3 months	7	No	—
1 year	3	No	—
Wants to meet a salesrep	10	Yes	10
Wants a quote	15	No	—
Total score			20

As the score increases, so the person moves up the sales ladder. A computer can easily keep track of the score. The weights can be established either through experience or by using regression techniques such as those described in Chapter 9.

THE TELEPHONE

'That's an amazing invention, but who would ever want to use one of them', said US President Rutherford Hayes about the telephone, in 1878.

Many sales offices and marketing departments have the same attitude. The telephone is still widely regarded with distrust. Telemarketing is often a dirty word, conjuring up images of double glazing and kitchen unit sales, and causing an immediate gut reaction: 'we're *not* doing telemarketing!'

Customer service is suffering as a direct consequence of neglect of the telephone. Like it or not, your customers and prospects will inevitably obtain your telephone number, and if you are not prepared, they will certainly not be completely satisfied when they call you.

PLANNING FOR INBOUND RESPONSES

Planning for incoming responses presents a unique combination of problems:

- you need costly telecoms equipment
- staffing levels will have to be increased
- there are forecasting difficulties associated with a reactive environment
- hitting the right balance between the mixed functions of sales and service is tricky.

The qualifications of telephone sales personnel must be different from those of service representatives and order takers:

- service people must be conciliatory, handling complaints, soothing heated tempers
- sales people need to fire up the buyer's enthusiasm, perhaps even encouraging them to buy a more expensive model
- order takers can sometimes be trained in tactful cross-selling and up-selling techniques, increasing the average order size.

Supervisory functions must not be neglected. It is common practice to have one supervisor to every eight people on the phone.

SYSTEMS REQUIREMENTS

Telephone response management can, if handled manually, bring with it a continuous problem of a surfeit of paper and a buzz of unanswered calls. Scripts, reports, information cards and telephone number files all mount up alarmingly in the course of just one week. A well-equipped operation should therefore be linked to a computer, with a screen for every operator, or a data-preparation team for support. (Relying on data preparation is not ideal when using a computer, but sometimes good communicators are incompetent at data entry, and so require some support.)

If telephone communicators can be trained in data entry, it is vital to ensure that adequate and comfortable headphones are provided so that both hands are free. It is important to give your staff a choice of models, and to involve them in the selection.

Call distribution for more than ten staff should be handled by a specialised piece of hardware called an ACD (or a modern PBX with ACD capabilities). This equipment distributes incoming calls evenly among telephone personnel and it tracks calls handled, wrap-up time and total talk time. It is vital for monitoring performance.

Calls on hold can be played a message. More modern units allow the caller to interact with them. Computerised voice synthesis and voice recognition are both being used commercially.

Hardware typically includes a mini- or microcomputer, with hard disk, and printers for producing follow-up letters. Interfaces with the ACD and the other operational computers may also be needed.

Software should be easy for non-computer people to use and remember:

- on-line help can be useful
- menus and/or function keys should be available for navigating round the system
- moving round the screen should be fast and flexible
- screen design should be suitable for long periods of viewing – use of colour should be well controlled
- window environments to display different types of data on screen simultaneously should be considered.

Technically, the software should include screen generators, script builders and report generators. An industry standard DBMS should be used, if possible. Transparent interfacing of the database to other corporate databases and to word-processors is desirable.

Integration is one of the big challenges. Data must be fed to other systems. Files containing responses may need to be sent to the sales force for follow-up. Alternatively, when customers place orders directly, direct access from the response handling system to the order processing system is required.

QUESTIONS

1 What is done with leads that are rejected/no sales?
(a) added to the database for later follow-up
(b) analysed to understand why they don't buy
(c) ignored or thrown away.

2 Have top management in your company ever posed as a customer with a complaint to test the follow-up system (or hired an outside consultancy to do the same?)

3 How often do top management see copies of or analyse customers' complaints?
(a) frequently
(b) occasionally
(c) rarely or never.

4

How do you use the telephone in marketing, sales and service?

(a) to take orders directly

(b) to fulfil requests for product information

(c) to identify the caller's nearest dealer

(d) to obtain demographic and psychographic information

(e) to screen credit

(f) to upgrade sales by suggesting additional products

(g) to quote prices

(h) to accept membership

(i) to set appointments

(j) to convert information calls to sales calls.

Follow-up

Time is money

That old proverb is very apt in sales and marketing. It can even be formulated as an equation:

Money = [Time with Customers] × [Customers with Money].

Time is one of the most misused of all resources. I have audited the quality of customer service provided by several organisations, and have found that, in many cases, customers were very dissatisfied because suppliers did not take the time to offer help and assistance.

More often than not, follow-up to customers' service requests is a disgrace to the name and reputation of the supplier. It makes me wonder who is responsible for creating such a poor impression when thousands or even millions of pounds have been spent on advertising to get the customer's interest. The following are the most common failures.

- Top of the list of customers' and prospects' complaints is no follow-up. For some companies, as many as 50 per cent of enquiries are not followed up.
- Slow follow-up is the next complaint. *Boardroom Reports* (15 September 1985) concluded that only 44 per cent of advertisers follow up enquiries prompted by ads or publicity releases within 60 days. About 17 per cent even fail to respond within 16 weeks.
- Poor follow-up is another common complaint. Letters are short, blunt and amateurish. Often the booklet that you requested is missing, or the information you wanted is only partially given. If you requested a visit, the representative can only call at an inconvenient time, and their attitude stinks when you ask for a better time. When they arrive (late, of course) they do not have the parts or information that you requested and they are rude.

These all too common problems anger customers and prospects. They result in lost revenues, lost customers and lost control. They also have associated hidden costs: duplication of effort, high travel costs and poor staff utilisation. They are symptomatic of more deep-rooted, debilitating management problems: poor morale, poor control management by crisis, exaggeration, misinformation and dishonesty.

While information systems will not provide a cure-all, if correctly used they can remove many of the causes of these problems.

TIME MANAGEMENT

The fate of any company engaged in selling hinges on its skill in harvesting sales revenue from prospective customers. Just as harvesting crops must be done at the right time, so must harvesting customers.

Time must have an active role in any sales and marketing system. The database, therefore, should contain lots of times and dates. The computer can read these times and be programmed to go 'beep', ring alarm bells, print letters, automatically telephone a customer or trigger a sales visit.

The database should contain times and dates specific to each individual customer or prospect: dates of past communications and transactions; times and dates for future events and planned activities. The database must have sufficient capacity to manage every contact, response and follow-up with all of these people.

For example, when an enquiry is received, by telephone or mail, the enquirer should be put on a particular follow-up plan. This will consist of one or more letters, calls or visits.

Or perhaps a contract needs to be renewed on a particular date. In that case, a month, a fortnight and a week before the contract expires, the customer should be sent a letter of reminder.

Each day the system should automatically produce the information needed to support all such follow-up actions. This may consist of letters, or it may be a call record, to remind the telemarketer to telephone a customer, or a 'tickler' record, to remind the sales representative to take action.

AUTOMATIC BRANCHED SCHEDULING

There is an art to sending the right message to the right person at the right time.

CASE EXAMPLE

Crown Paints found that their enquirers fell into two camps: those who proposed to decorate (and hence purchase) almost immediately, and those who were planning some months ahead. An entirely different follow-up procedure was appropriate to each group. Also, the cost of follow-up was different. Those who were going to purchase almost immediately warranted the more expensive follow-up.

A branching follow-up schedule, as shown in Figure 13.1, is often important for managing a dialogue with different types of people with different needs. Some software packages can help automate such branched schedules. The software identifies which branch is most appropriate to each individual, and automatically records the dates and actions on that person's record. When the action is due, the system automatically prints the letter, or prompts the reminder or tickler.

AVOIDING THE ACTIVITY TRAP

Automation of scheduling is only practical for the simpler types of follow-up activity. For most salesforces, it is one of the key responsibilities of the people themselves to schedule activities.

Studies of sales activity have shown that sales reps often manage their schedules poorly, and get trapped into performing certain routine activities. For example, they may habitually visit certain customers merely as a courtesy.

Methods of managing time have been developed by companies such as Time Manager International, and these techniques have now been embodied in a number of software packages.

The concept is very simple – bridging what you want to do and when you want to do it. Unlike simple diary management software, which simply helps to avoid missed deadlines and other inefficiencies, the aim of time management is to be more effective. Doing the right things, as well as doing things at the right time.

Sophisticated time management systems focus on key results. Software is useful in this regard, since it can be used to take an overview of a detailed diary, and can check that activities are aimed at key results. 'To do' lists can be produced, and the setting of priorities and deadlines facilitated. Overall goals can be broken down into key areas, tasks and activities.

THE FOLLOW-UP TARGET

Who should be followed up? How should follow-up be targeted?

The right answer is that *all* sales responses should receive some follow-up acknowledgement, simply as a matter of courtesy. Also, research shows that about half of all respondents to advertisements will buy within a year. So some persistence in following these up will pay dividends. Usually it takes time to condition customers to be receptive to your product.

Of course, this advice cannot be taken if the responses are not recorded in the first place. A survey of follow-ups to mortgage enquiries, in the

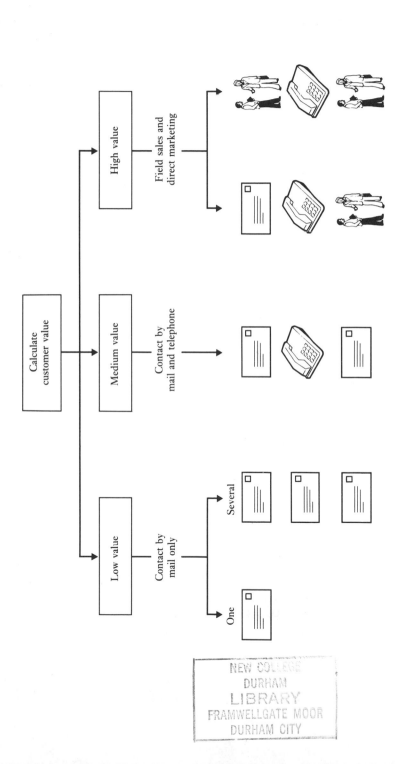

Figure 13.1 Optimum follow-up management assigns high-cost follow-up to high-value customers and low-cost follow-up to low-value customers.

UK, revealed that fewer than 20 per cent of banks and building societies take the opportunity to build a prospect list by recording details of the enquiry. Staff working on the counters were generally not trained to record such details.

Another problem that must be overcome is the salesforce's 'winner mentality'. Most sales representatives are trained in a very macho way, and focus most of their attention on winning. When they get a prospect, they work very hard at persuading that individual to buy. Usually about 4 per cent will quickly convert to 'Wins', but the remaining 96 per cent will be viewed as 'Losses', and cease to be of interest. Yet a third of them would have been close to being persuaded, and would have converted to Wins over time. Another third might have been persuaded, if they had heard something more relevant to their needs. (See Figure 13.2.) The challenge is to get the salesforce to record these non-Wins for follow-up action.

TOOLS TO HELP FOLLOW-UP

Because time is of the essence, the good sales representative is always well organised. Information systems can provide useful tools to help organise the follow-up action.

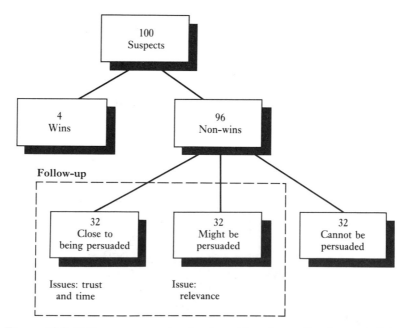

Figure 13.2 Follow up suspects who do not buy immediately to condition them to be more receptive to buying in future.

Laptop computers can be useful. They help keep on hand all the materials to bring the prospect and the sale together: order forms, sales slips, purchase orders, selling materials and specification sheets. They must be organised and ready to use.

SoftAd is one company who produce animated sales aids to run on laptop computers. They helped one pharmaceuticals company who were selling an arthritis treatment. The software allowed the rep to answer a wide range of technical questions, and even included animated pictures of bone joints, demonstrating why the treatment was superior to its competitors.

A TYPICAL WORKING DAY

Picture the following scenario.

8:05 a.m. You are in a hotel in John O'Groats, the day after the annual sales conference. You log onto the company's computer system, using your portable computer with telephone modem and ask for messages, if any.

8:06 a.m. Memo from the MD, 'Need your estimates by region and product line no later than two weeks. Need rough figures tomorrow, 9 a.m. Thanks.'

8:07 a.m. Memo from market research. 'Competitor X has introduced its three pack in a test market, as we thought. Believe we may be vulnerable. Will keep you informed.'

8:12 a.m. Prepare for the day's calls. Look up notes on visits due this week. You see that you stand a chance of winning the sales contest if you close the deal with one of the customers today.

8:15 a.m. Review notes of previous visits to the customer. See that there were problems with part shipments for the last three orders, and the customer is getting annoyed.

10:38 a.m. Arrive at first appointment of the day, after two hour drive, and are 20 minutes early. Sort out expense receipts using the laptop to do expense report. Store the data for later transmission.

10:59 a.m. Called in by the buyer. Walk round his area of the store, and take note of stock. Seeing that two items not stocked are on approved-to-buy list, agree order, and enter on laptop.

11:30 a.m. Meet store manager. Print order for signed approval.

11:35 a.m. Use computer to transmit order. Enter notes on competitor's new product seen in store. Enter information on your call report. Store for later transmission.

12:10 p.m. Lunch. You note that you have some time available in the afternoon, and log onto computer to examine any new enquiries from prospects you might visit. Note name and address, and call to make an appointment. At this time, you transmit all information about the morning's activity to HQ's computer.

1:30 p.m. Arriving ahead of time, at difficult key account, note that competitor has begun its annual promotion campaign two weeks early. Transmit urgent message to request extension to promotion period for this account.

1:40 p.m. Message received authorising extension of promotion. Review details of problem customer's account.

2:30 p.m. Make contact with problem customer. Ask reasons for fall off in business. Customer replies, 'your prices are out of line'. Extend promotion and get order. Note complaint for call report.

2:50 p.m. Back in the car, transmit the order. This could make you the winner of the sales competition.

4:40 p.m. Arrive at branch sales office. Check database for possible prospects for the rest of the week, and check credit ratings. Two are excellent, one not acceptable. See one has opened a new location, indicating growth. Call and make appointments.

5:30 p.m. Check electronic mail. Log off for the day.

THE COMMUNICATIONS REVOLUTION

Communications is an important aspect of the follow-up process for a travelling salesforce. A number of new inventions have found their way into the salesrep's car or briefcase, but only a few have given the lasting benefits claimed by their inventors.

The ability to communicate on the move is nothing new. In 1903 the British Army used radio for manoeuvres. And it is 30 years since British Telecom (then the Post Office) launched a mobile telephone service for a handful of privileged customers. That handful grew steadily until 1985, when the new cellular services were launched. Today over 500,000 people in the UK use cellular phones.

Another service, which is less expensive than cellular but only offers one-way communication, is radio paging. Today there are over 500,000 pagers in the UK. They can send a lengthy message to the field, as well as simply buzzing for attention. Voice messaging and voice mail solve the problem of the busy line. Messages can be stored and transmitted even when the line is busy.

A common problem is not knowing where to find the representative. However, the day is not far away when everyone will have a simple pocket-sized communications terminal that can be carried anywhere. It could be used as a phone, pager or as a messaging service. Whatever it is used for, everyone will be contacted via their own number. This number will not only be valid in the UK; Europe and North America could also be in the network, which will support data communications as well as voice. This is called 'personal communications', i.e. contacting people rather than places.

The international cooperation that exists in the communications marketplace is steadily leading to a common standard. By the late 1990s, a common system of personal communications will be in operation throughout much of the world.

These days, communications are as much about data as voice. Currently only 1 per cent of mobile communication customers use data as well as voice, but the numbers are increasing.

The BBC used a British Telecom datalink at Wimbledon during the tennis championships to sell studio time and computer graphics to organisations throughout the world. With all the bad weather problems that Wimbledon experiences, it was vital that this sort of operation was carried out from the location, not from a remote studio.

Although this was a specialised application, a sales rep on the road could use similar communications methods to check on computer records. British Telecom predicts that within two years 10 per cent of all mobile communications users will transmit data, and that the numbers will continue to grow till the turn of the century.

QUESTIONS

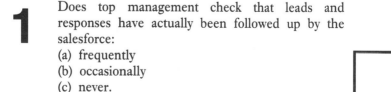

1 Does top management check that leads and responses have actually been followed up by the salesforce:
(a) frequently
(b) occasionally
(c) never.

2 Where leads are rejected by the salesforce as too poor in quality to justify a follow-up, how do you review the situation to improve lead quality?
(a) research a sample of poor leads to understand the problem
(b) pass the leads to a different salesman to find whether they are more successful
(c) do nothing.

3 How often do top management see how complaints are followed up?
(a) frequently
(b) occasionally
(c) rarely or never.

4 What level of tools do you provide to improve the way in which each salesperson plans his or her time in the week and month ahead?
(a) effective sales tools
(b) rudimentary tools
(c) no tools.

5 Can your salesforce communicate as quickly and efficiently from the field as they need?

Monitoring

I was seldom able to see an opportunity until it had ceased to be one.

Mark Twain

THE BAD DREAM

Perhaps more than anyone else, sales and marketing managers are being inundated by data. Sales information is flooding in faster and faster, threatening to engulf the sales manager in a tidal wave of computer print-outs. It sounds like a bad dream but it is quickly becoming a reality.

Right now, a product manager gets periodic reports from the computer that contain about 100,000 new numbers every time. It has become practically impossible for a manager to assimilate all the data available. Opportunities are being missed within the marketplace, and managers are constantly searching for gems of information. It is like looking for a needle in a haystack.

Sales and marketing is about exploration. You sift through a lot of data to find new truths, to try to understand what causes things, and to see what the implications are. But what managers need to look at is exceptional data, not the normal stuff.

Managers must be supplied with accurate, easy-to-understand information about their actions and the market's response to them. They must be supplied with information in time to correct any serious problems.

A complete monitoring and reporting system consists of several integrated applications, each of which meets a particular management need. The major applications are

- Executive Information Systems
- key factor reporting
- responsibility reporting
- cost reporting.

EXECUTIVE INFORMATION SYSTEMS

With the older generation of systems, managers had to sort through 100 per cent of the data to identify the best 10 per cent and the worst 10 per cent. The newer solution is either to build an Executive Information System (EIS), or to hire a lot of people to look through the fine detail.

Software packages, such as Comshare's System W, and EXECUCOM and PILOT, are widely used for EISs. The Centre for Information Systems Research at MIT conducted a telephone survey of Fortune 500 companies and found that over 50 per cent had an active EIS in place with high or moderate use.

This means that senior management were accessing on-line reports summarising their position and trends that would change their position. By automating the monitoring of transactions, the new EISs are able to provide up-to-date accurate information to those people traditionally starved of it: senior management. The philosophy behind EIS is that information is only as good as the data behind it: i.e. an EIS is only as good as the data behind it. That data must have the right structure, in order for the EIS to work. Figure 14.1 shows a typical EIS data structure.

For top-level corporate control, executives need to be provided with a menu of simple standard reports, showing the current situation, trends and problems. This is the EIS layer. It contains well-structured relevant information, but no detailed data.

The source of the EIS information is, however, the detailed Decision Support System (DSS) database. Information from this is carefully structured, filtered and organised before it goes to the EIS layer. The DSS database contains details of all transactions, such as campaigns, costs, budgets, contacts, responses, orders, prices, discounts, etc. This data is drawn into the DSS database from the more detailed data produced by transaction systems, which might include cost accounting systems, campaign planning, direct marketing or field sales systems.

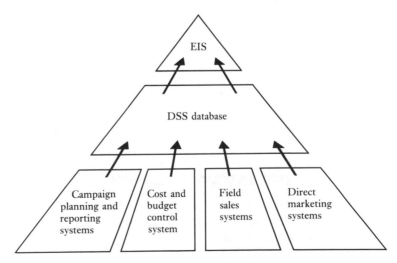

Figure 14.1 **Data needs to be arranged hierarchically in EISs and DSSs.**

The new generation of EISs provide two important capabilities for the busy senior executive:

- *Traffic light reporting.* The system highlights what is important, and filters out what isn't. The rules for deciding what to show, and what not to, are based on a tolerance range set when the system is developed. Using colours helps the busy executive to speed-read: red means stop (problem), yellow means caution (problem ahead) and green means go!
- *Drill down.* Where there are problems, the system allows the manager to drill through the layers of information – starting with high-level EIS, moving through progressively more detailed information, until eventually finding the specific detail in the DSS database that was causing the problem. Thus, a cost overrun shown in the EIS might be tracked down to an invoice that had been incorrectly allocated when it was entered into the accounting systems. With drill-down reporting, the problem can be isolated and quickly corrected.

CASE EXAMPLE – CONSUMER PRODUCTS

The ability to monitor the success of a campaign in terms of product sales and market share is vitally important for managing the huge advertising and promotional spends in the notoriously fickle beer industry. Scottish and Newcastle recognised that they were being bombarded with masses of information that was difficult to use – from sales orders, field intelligence and external market research – and chose an EIS to assist them. The EIS chosen was selected because of its flexibility: it could run on PCs, minicomputers and mainframes.

The design was rigorous. Data was highly complex and warranted data analysis. Within Scottish and Newcastle's marketplace there are sectors, majors, minors, groups, TV areas and regions, brands, packs, volumes, weeks, periods, years. Add to this sales estimates for competitors' brands, advertising data, pricing and promotions, and you can see the extent of the data design problem.

The problem of aggregation of data was solved, using the philosophy illustrated in Figure 14.1. High-level aggregation was provided for the top executives. These were classified as 'button pushers' and 'selectors'. Button pushers needed rapid training and encouragement to push buttons and try things out, while selectors were more inquisitive.

User acceptance of the system was high. Sales management are pleased with the new formats of report they receive. They can easily make comparisons, using data fused together from Neilsen, Stats MR and in-house sources, and can answer their sales and marketing enquiries much faster and much more objectively than before, using their own desk-top equipment.

MANUAL SUPPORT

About 50 per cent of large companies, and even more medium and small companies, do not have EIS. They traditionally turn to outside agencies to measure their efforts.

What do they measure? There is no simple answer – a recent survey revealed at least ten very different measures being applied to sales promotion campaigns alone. No systematic measures seemed to be applied.

Over 75 per cent of those surveyed recorded numbers of people responding to their campaigns; yet many of these did not measure the number of sales resulting. Almost 40 per cent used qualitative research to measure their effectiveness; only 20 per cent used quantitative research. Some relied on informal feedback from the salesforce; others trusted their agency to tell them how effective they were.

Haphazard manual measurement is all too commonplace. However, the identification of key factors, and their systematic reporting, is beginning to replace yesterday's chaos.

KEY FACTOR REPORTING

Key factor reporting involves the automatic identification, by the monitoring systems of the half dozen key factors that should be brought to the attention of each senior manager, and the distribution of individual reports tailored to each person's needs. Minimal manual effort should be needed to view these figures.

Who benefits from such an approach? Head office sales management can see where sales are on target, and can locate problems. Though in their previous systems they may have already received this data, it was usually buried in computer output. Data that was formerly transmitted slowly and inefficiently becomes quicker and easier to view. A recent survey revealed the sales reporting practices of companies in the USA (see Table 14.1).

Table 14.1 Management reports generated by support systems

Type of report	Percentage of companies using it
Customer account activity and status	89
Sales or orders summaries	58
Sales in process, bids outstanding	56
Selling expenses	49
Salesperson's call activities	36
Exceptional situations status	31
Competitive activity	29

Head office marketing management can see whether a particular brand is on target and locate problems. Responses to direct marketing or sales promotion campaigns can be tracked, and low results can be spotted so that the campaigns or their fulfilment can be adjusted. For example, the results shown in Figure 14.2 indicate that:

- responses are 20 per cent ahead of forecast: the printers may need to be warned in case more literature needs to be printed
- sales are 10 per cent below forecast: the key factor report in Figure 14.3 shows why.

Two different 'test' offers have resulted in this situation. The first, offering a high incentive to respond has generated many responses, and a high response rate. However, the responses were of poor quality, resulting in a lower than average sales conversion rate. The second, lower, incentive has produced a lower, but still satisfactory, response rate; however, these responses were of high quality, and resulted in a high sales conversion rate.

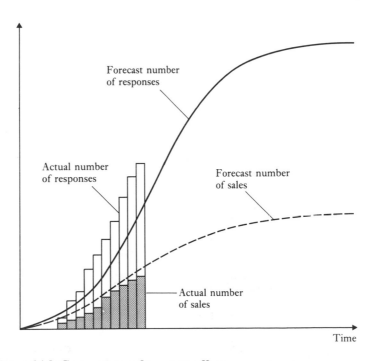

Figure 14.2 Comparison of two test offers.

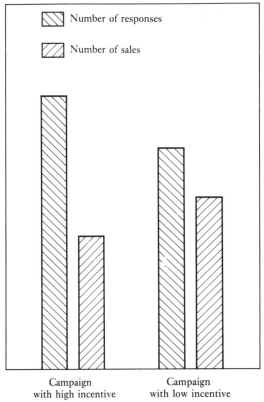

Figure 14.3 **Monitoring of campaign performance.**

RESPONSIBILITY REPORTING

Monitoring and reporting should not be the exclusive domain of senior management. Everyone is responsible for delivering a part, however small, of the plans described in Chapter 10.

Responsibility reporting monitors the results of actual performance against planned performance. This is done in such a way that deviations from plan can be related to the *specific individual responsible* for controlling such deviations. In addition, responsibility reporting systems provide enough detail regarding deviations to assist in pinpointing the causal factors.

The techniques of responsibility reporting are deceptively simple. Properly developed and installed, however, a system of responsibility reporting is one of the most powerful management control devices available.

It is distinguished from the typical departmental reporting system in that it reflects only those revenues, costs and activities that are controlled by the manager (e.g. advertising and promotion costs): departmental reports often include factors that are beyond the department's control (e.g. manufacturing costs might appear in a brand manager's departmental reports).

Responsibility reporting tailors the information to show factors that are controlled by a single person, and maintains that integrity throughout the reporting levels (for example, it may show outstanding invoices, or leads not followed up). Departmental reporting on the other hand reflects the composite efforts of a number of managers.

A responsibility reporting system requires a clear definition of responsibilities and reporting relationships. The clarification of these is an important prerequisite of a successful responsibility reporting system.

CASE EXAMPLE – CONSUMER DURABLES DEALER RESPONSIBILITY REPORTING

This motor vehicle manufacturer sells vehicles, service and spare parts through dealers. The dealers give customers a choice of competing vehicles, so it is important for the manufacturer to measure and influence customer satisfaction and competitive position. The programme involves mailing questionnaires to all private passenger car customers of all participating dealers, at 2 months after purchase and again at 24 months. The results are fed back into the database, and analysed to determine:

- customer satisfaction (see Table 14.2)
- dealer performance (see Table 14.3).

Table 14.2 Customer satisfaction report

Dissatisfied owners	Problem
Mr John Smith 59 Winford Way Chiswick London W4 2LH 081–995 7672	Dissatisfied with service department Vehicle prep problems Would not recommend salesperson/dealer
Ms Jane Williams 34 High Street Chiswick London W4 3TH 081–994 1345	Vehicle prep problems Dissatisfied with sales department Very dissatisfied with dealership overall

Dealers then contact customers who are not satisfied. The second type of report is used by the manufacturer's representative when counselling the dealer.

Table 14.3 Dealer satisfaction index

Issue	Your results	Your district	League position
Sales courteous	6.98	8.28	45/50
Test drive offered	66%	89%	47/50
Service contract offered	69%	92%	48/50
Appearance	5.78	7.77	43/50
Service quality	4.45	6.54	50/50

These scores indicate that the dealer is near the bottom of their league. Sales are discourteous, a test drive is often not offered, service contracts are often not offered, appearance is poor and service quality very poor.

Some dealerships may be cancelled as a result of such results. The good news is that the manufacturer has all the names and addresses of customers, and can write to them to alert them of the change.

COST ACCOUNTING

Costs underlie many of the monitoring needs of sales and marketing. Yet, sadly, cost information is rarely recorded in a useful way.

Cost accounting should meet the needs of all functions – including sales and marketing – not just finance. Traditionally, cost accounting methods have mainly been applied to factories and manufacturing facilities. However, with today's costs of marketing and selling receiving more and more attention, cost accounting methods have become useful in many sales and marketing decisions. For example:

- evaluation of selling prices
- make or buy decisions
- media choice
- list testing
- copy testing.

While accurate cost information is always required, the combinations of costs, margins or contributions will require a slightly different definition in each case – a definition that is driven by the needs of sales and marketing.

For example, in evaluating selling prices, sales managers need to know the difference between sales price and full product cost, including all costs directly attributable to the product plus indirect costs. In the case of a make or buy decision, marketing managers need to know the direct manufacturing cost only.

These examples serve to illustrate the importance of understanding the management uses for cost information, prior to designing the cost accounting system. In addition to providing information for finance, cost accounting systems also provide the basic data necessary for sales and marketing to do responsibility reporting, key factor reporting and EIS.

LINKING MONITORING BACK TO ANALYSIS

We complete the virtuous circle by linking back to where we started. Armed with the information produced by monitoring, we look for problems to analyse. For example, the costs per lead produced by four alternative advertisements (copy A, B, C, D) and three different mailing lists might be monitored (see Table 14.4).

Table 14.4 **Comparison of the effectiveness of different advertisements and mailing lists**

| | Cost per lead ($£$) | | | | |
	Copy A	Copy B	Copy C	Copy D	Average
List 1	44	56	32	80	53
List 2	50	62	46	90	62
List 3	32	53	45	70	50
Average	42	57	41	80	55

This report indicates that List 2 is the best, List 1 next best and List 3 performs the worst. It also indicates that Copy D is the best, Copy B next best, Copy A next, closely followed by Copy C.

This monitoring shows strengths and weaknesses, but it gives no explanation. In order to explain the differences, research and analysis will be needed. And so another cycle begins.

QUESTIONS

 1

How comprehensive is your capability for monitoring mistakes and making sure they never recur?
(a) very comprehensive
(b) patchy
(c) nonexistent.

2 How quickly are last week's results consolidated and communicated to top management?
(a) within one day
(b) within one week
(c) a month or more.

3 Do you know what the controls that really matter to you and your employees really are. How well are they being measured?
(a) too much detail
(b) too little detail
(c) too late
(d) too inflexible
(e) just right.

4 What financial information is monitored on a regular basis?
(a) revenues
(b) some costs
(c) all costs
(d) profitability
(e) none of the above.

5 Do you measure the current performance of each salesperson, both by results and by activity?

6 Do you monitor by sales territory the effectiveness of direct marketing and sales promotion in generating leads for your salespeople?

7 Do you keep track of what happened to last month's best bets?

8 Do you have accurate early warning of products, services and markets that are on the way out or on the way in?

9 Can you spot and avoid looming catastrophes?

10 Can you produce individual performance ratios and company norm ratios each quarter, and use these to set specific performance improvement targets for the next quarter?

11 Do you use the performance ratios to pinpoint individual training and retraining needs?

Customer Databases

There are just two kinds of data, the kind you look up and the kind you make up.

Rex Stout (1969)

WHAT IS A DATABASE?

In their current enthusiasm for 'database' marketing, marketing and sales management often pass over the question of what a database really is. Their use of the word certainly differs from that of computing professionals, who use 'database' to describe certain kinds of software which provide linkages between different items of information.

A database can be properly defined as follows: a collection of related data stored together, with the minimum of duplication and providing a common pool of information to serve one or more applications. Hence the database is the information itself, not the software or tools used to manage and manipulate the information.

With database software called a Database Management System (DBMS) you can link data together in relational or hierarchical structures allowing fast and efficient access to particular fields, without having to process the entire file.

In popular terms, the adoption of a database means putting all the sales and marketing organisation's data into one computerised filing system. However, in practice it can also mean assembling a number of separate databases, each serving a group of related applications. It can be perfectly acceptable to have several databases coexisting. Thus we may find organisations with different needs following a variety of approaches:

- a mail order company may have a single database, serving direct mail and order processing applications
- a building society may have two separate databases, one dealing with direct mail and one with mortgage accounting.
- a computer company may have several databases, interlinked, covering direct mail, telemarketing, field sales and order processing.

Obviously where more than one database is involved, it may be necessary to provide bridges, or *interfaces*, for data to flow between them.

THE NEED TO ADOPT A DATABASE APPROACH

Adopting a database approach can be expensive in the short term. Therefore you need to be sure that the arguments for doing so are valid and
can be justified in an objective fashion. Suppliers and computer staff
may advance technical arguments for a database approach that sound
convincing, but its adoption may be more beneficial to them than to the
organisation as a whole. (By the same token, your salesforce might argue
that the allocation of Rolls-Royce rather than a fleet car would make
them more effective.)

The reasons for adopting the database approach are a mixture of
technical factors and user requirements.

- *Duplication* of data can be reduced or eliminated by the database
  approach. For example, customer records may be repeated several
  times in records used for different purposes, such as order
  processing, accounts receivable, credit control and direct mail, and
  the same product details may appear dozens or even hundreds of
  times in different files. A database approach will be designed to
  eliminate redundant data and so reduce the wastage of storage space
  and processing.
- *Inconsistency* of data is a more significant problem from a user's point
  of view. Although almost identical records may exist, the separation
  of files and applications can mean that they are updated at different
  times, and are recorded and stored in different formats. For
  example, a consumer product might be recorded half a dozen
  different ways, as shown in Table 15.1.

Table 15.1   **Different ways that one product may be recorded**

Data	Comment
Domestica 70cl	As described for order processing
Domestica bott	As defined for sales history
Domest e.q.	For accounting purposes, converted to 75cl equiv-alent cases (e.q.)
DOM070	Coded for the Marketing Information System
100456	The product number that appears in the price list, and is used by the salesforce
DOM070/P2	The warehousing number, showing the 'bottle-neck' promotion for this batch

When data is held separately under each product code or description,
it is possible for six different prices to be held simultaneously.

- *Inflexibility* characterises many non-database practices. Often an interpretation of codes is embedded in the computer programs that operate them. If you wish to amend or add to the file or record structure, you may have to change the parameters for every program that utilises the file. This could mean altering dozens of programs, recompiling and testing them – hoping you have not caused other problems. This accounts in part for the anguish with which a computer manager greets any user request for change, and why it takes an apparently disproportionate amount of time to introduce what appears to be a simple change. One of the great advantages of the database approach is that it provides the facility to insulate programs from data, and allows modifications of databases with minimal changes to existing systems.

Today it is safe to say that a database approach is worth considering for new systems. However, this may entail the new sales and marketing systems being built with a database approach, while the existing systems remain non-database – with interfaces feeding the marketing databases from existing systems.

PROBLEMS WITH INTEGRATING EXISTING APPLICATIONS

The question of how to achieve an integrated database brings to mind the old joke:

Question: 'How do I get to Dublin from here?'
Answer: 'If I was heading for Dublin I wouldn't have started from here.'

In an ideal world, one would totally integrate all databases. This would mean that existing operational systems, such as order processing, credit control or accounts receivable, could benefit from the database approach, and share the same data as the sales and marketing systems.

However, in practice such a high degree of integration would be costly and technically difficult. Consequently, the totally integrated strategy should not normally be the first objective of any database builder. Rather, the fusion strategy described in Chapter 4 should be adopted. While this means that two sets of databases are developed – marketing and operational – significant benefits can be realised without the high cost of total integration.

The costs of total integration accrue from many areas:

- purchasing and developing hardware and software
- designing the new operational databases
- converting existing operational systems to work under the database regime

- the disruption caused to daily operations by moving across to the new database regime.

These costs can be prohibitive unless there are substantial benefits of the database approach to operational staff. Under most circumstances, it is wiser to take a smaller step towards a marketing database, before redeveloping the operational systems.

THE NEED FOR A DBMS

Just as a database approach is often advocated as a cure-all for the ills of existing systems, so too is the similar sounding Database Management System or DBMS.

One of the problems with DBMSs is that they are intellectually challenging. They become objects of interest in their own right. I have met many people, from data processing and marketing alike, who are clearly fascinated by them. They tell me proudly about the differences between 'relational' and 'hierarchical' structures. They develop 'data models' – lofty structures of breathtakingly abstract complexity.

Yet it is often difficult for management to identify the direct benefits to the user of a DBMS approach, especially when most of the arguments advanced appear to be advantageous to the data processing department:

- better use of facilities
- ease of change and maintenance
- an exciting new technique to attract and retain the interests of the computer expert.

The first time sales or marketing managers hear about DBMSs and their advantages is when a proposal from the computer department lands on the desk. Just as they are beginning to learn about computers, they are plunged into a new and baffling area of jargon and expertise that places them once more at the mercy of the technician.

This is not the place to give you a lay person's introduction to database jargon: there are many such books in print today.

However, I advise you not to place your trust totally in the technicians. You should make sure that they are basing their decisions on sound commercial judgement, particularly with regards to three questions:

- Will the DBMS provide information to users' satisfaction?
- Will it do the jobs that users expect?
- Will its operation be within the capabilities of your people?

Not all DBMSs have the same end-user capabilities. Some systems, such as Oracle and Ingres, include tools that allow end-users to manipulate data and create reports and outputs without substantial help from data processing. But doing the job means much more than just end-user tools. Capabilities to examine closely are:

- data distribution capabilities
- multiple operating systems
- multi-hardware support (where you have several different hardware environments)
- performance of batch and on-line processes.

Several DBMSs are becoming capable of manipulating data held at different locations in a manner that is clear to the end-user. Additions, deletions and updates, multiple copies and other functions, which can lead to data integrity problems in distributed databases, are handled without error by some modern DBMSs.

Where you are using multiple operating systems (such as UNIX, MVS, DOS, VMS, OS/2) or multiple hardwares (such as IBM 30XX, IBM 43XX, IBM AS/400, DEC VAX, ICL, UNISYS, HP, BULL, NCR, Data General, Apple) you need to be careful to ensure that the DBMS you have chosen will work throughout your systems.

Performance of DBMSs is still a problem. Table 15.2 illustrates the trade-off between several types.

Table 15.2 Comparison of different types of DBMS

	Relational	Type of DBMS Hierarchical	Flat file
Examples	DB2, Oracle	IMS	VSAM
Language	Universal (SQL)	Specific	Specific
Programmer productivity	High	Medium	Low
Machine performance	Low	Medium	High

As one moves from flat file to hierarchical to relational databases, the speed with which the data processing department can modify and maintain the systems increases. However, the trade-off is reduced DBMS performance.

The performance of a computer system is measured in terms of the time (and hence cost) of performing a given set of instructions, invoked by the applications being run. The time is taken by two activities:

- storing and retrieving data (essentially the time taken by the data-retrieval arm in the disk pack – known as input/output or I/O time)
- performing instructions (known as Central Processing Unit or CPU time).

The following formulae can be used as first gross estimates:

$$\text{CPU Time} = \frac{\text{Total Instructions/Exchange}}{\text{CPU Speed (in instructions per second)}}$$

I/O Time = Accesses/Exchange × (Seek + Rotation + Data Transfer).

Other factors, such as contention elongation are then taken into account in arriving at the figures for on-line response time and batch processing time.

While you need not perform such calculations yourself, you must ensure that the data processing management have done them, before you start to develop your database. Sadly, surprisingly few database developments take heed of such precautions.

DATA ADMINISTRATORS

Unplanned or ill-conceived deployment of a company's information assets wastes time and money. Effective information asset management is a skilled task. Many companies recognise this by appointing a data administrator, who is responsible for:

- collecting, storing and distributing data
- data quality management
- 'traffic' control of database access
- support and advice for information users
- cost and activity reporting.

To guarantee the quality of the data, the information must be entered in a standard format, audited and, where problems exist, cleaned.

Although these tasks were once the responsibility of the DP department, the advent of the on-line monitor, or visual display unit (VDU), led to a shift of responsibility to the end-user. Today that change has occurred on a large scale, and few DP departments have any responsibility for data itself.

The solution for sales and marketing management is to appoint a data administrator to maintain the quality of the data they use. This person may be a member of sales or marketing, or may be in the DP department.

SPECIFYING DATA TO RETAIN

An important task is to decide what information to retain. One of the first steps should be to review existing information usage and needs. The outcome is a definition of information requirements, which may in some instances be quite different from the information currently provided. Not only will some components be missing, but others will need cutting back. For example, data that is:

* no longer accurate
* no longer wanted
* not used.

The review will also show where users are not exploiting existing data. This may be an educational problem, or it may be due to poor quality of the data.

Information requirements usually split into two areas:

* passive data
* active data.

Passive data is collected from existing sources such as:

* customer details
* orders taken
* service utilisation
* products purchased
* prices given
* discounts given.

This information is assembled to answer historical questions, such as:

* Who bought what, where and when?
* What did who buy where and when?
* Where did who buy what and when?
* When did who buy what and where?

Do not expect such data to hold all the answers you are seeking. It often only contains accounts receivable data, focusing on those who pay the bill, not those who make buying decisions.

Active data must be added to answer future questions, such as:

* Who will buy what, where and when?
* What will who buy where and when?

- Where will who buy what and when?
- When will who buy what and where?

The relational nature of today's databases readily lends itself to these types of flexible problems. The data is shown schematically in Figure 15.1.

Brainstorming is an important technique to use when specifying data to be retained. A brainstorming session should be used to select all potentially useful passive data, and to imagine all sources of active data. Creativity is the key.

After the brainstorming is over, priorities should be set. Think about

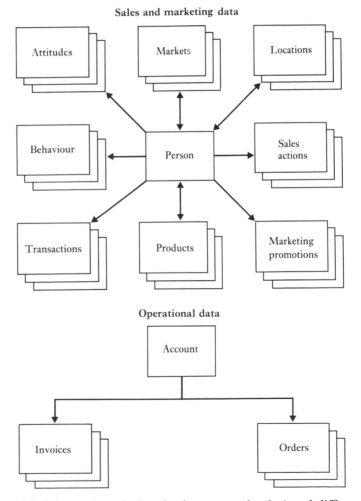

Figure 15.1 Sales and marketing databases must be designed differently from operational databases.

the benefits of having information. Plan the outputs, reports and methods of accessing the data. Beware of information for information's sake.

QUESTIONS

1 How well informed are you about customers, their spending habits and propensity to spend?
(a) fully informed
(b) there are some gaps in my knowledge
(c) major holes exist in my knowledge.

2 Are you often frustrated because different information sources conflict? How many sources of data do you have at present?
(a) one perfect source of data
(b) one imperfect source
(c) two to five different sources of data
(d) more than five
(e) don't know.

3 Are old outdated databases maintained long after they were due to be shut down?

4 What are the weaknesses in your data administration?
(a) too much data
(b) too little data
(c) too outdated
(d) too approximate
(e) too inaccurate.

5 What problems do you experience when pulling together the information that you need?
(a) too many sources
(b) do not have tools to collate data
(c) no problems.

Part III Getting Results

The ABC of Innovation

Debbie Moore, boss of dance and fashion company Pineapple, confessed recently that ignorance of computers had caused her to waste £100,000 on a computer system that did not meet her needs . . . despite doubts, she felt unable to challenge her experts 'and left them to get on with it'.

Business *(May 1990)*

Why not hand over to the technical experts and let them get on with it? Surely getting a system is rather like buying a new car or a building? You don't need to be an engineer or an architect to buy a car or a building! Part III of this book considers how to get results.

To answer these questions, consider first the differences between buying a car and a building. With a car, you are selecting something with very simple properties – speed, comfort and beauty in the eyes of the beholder. Within these simple parameters, mass production of thousands of different models is possible. Any modification of mass production models is, however, usually minor and cosmetic. Few car buyers today would consider engaging a team of engineers to get what they want.

With a building, you are selecting something not quite so simple. It is commonplace to engage experts – architects, surveyors, plumbers, electricians, plasterers, carpenters and other technical specialists – and to spend considerable periods of time in discussion with them, in order to get what you want. The larger or more complex the building, the more important it is that you engage a competent architect; one who speaks English not jargon.

Systems are more like buildings than cars. It is necessary for you to spend time discussing what you want with the systems managers, and any other specialists, to be confident of results. It is also necessary for other people who will be using the system to discuss their needs and wants – you will have to set priorities and make compromises to sort out any conflicts between the needs of different users.

With systems, your problems begin when you start looking for someone who fulfils the architect's role. You need to communicate in English, not computerspeak: this is apparently rather difficult for many systems specialists. But there is worse to come.

THERE IS NOBODY TO COPY ANYMORE

Sales and marketing often learn by example, or from past successes. This is not possible with computers in sales and marketing: innovation is the challenge.

Unfortunately, systems specialists, DP managers and IT experts tend to be very conservative and very poor innovators. They tend to offer users the familiar and the tried and tested technologies. So who will lead the innovation?

Look at the innovations of the 1980s: personal computers, word-processing, facsimile machines, desktop publishing, spreadsheets. All these worked as a direct result of user demand – often in spite of the efforts of hidebound DP management.

While there is no recipe for success in areas of businesses which have resisted computerisation, there are some useful dos and don'ts.

- *Do* ensure that every sales and marketing manager knows the answer to the question: 'what impact will information systems have on my sales and marketing strategy?' The answer may be 'none at all', although I personally doubt it. The point is that to ignore information systems in the face of all the evidence around us today amounts to a dereliction of duty.
- *Don't* forget that computerising sales and marketing requires innovation. It will not be like the traditional areas – accounting, factory automation, warehousing, distribution, transaction systems – where successful methodologies for system building exist. If you attempt to apply those methods to sales and marketing you will be courting disaster.
- *Don't* hand over all responsibility for innovation to your DP people. They are often slaves to methodologies such as Hoskyns PRISM, Andersen Consulting's Method/1 or SSADM. These rule books for systems builders are there to protect your DP staff from risk. They may work well in known areas, such as accounting, but should not be applied mindlessly to more innovative areas. Methodologies tend to suffocate innovation rather than nurture it. The reason is that they concentrate on simply *building* a system. They tell you to employ analysts, to interview 'users' and determine their 'requirements'. However, there are no 'users' for systems that do not yet exist. There are no 'requirements'. Vision is needed to design innovative systems, and methodologies have little to say about creating vision. Figure 16.1 highlights the differences between the innovative approach and the traditional. In a traditional function, the culture determines the systems used, whereas in an innovative area, there is a two-way flow of ideas. In an innovative area, the

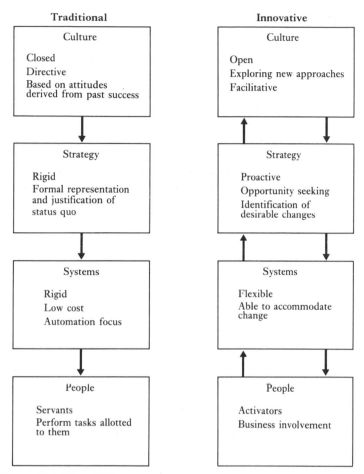

Figure 16.1 The ABC stages.

systems are affected by the culture and the strategy, but also the systems affect the culture and the strategy. The innovative environment is much more fluid, and the systems have to be correspondingly more flexible.

- *Don't* expect anyone to have perfect 20:20 vision. Adjustments must inevitably be made to any new system, after it has been built.
- *Do* allocate budgets and resources to enhance and maintain the new systems.
- *Do* actively seek commitment from those who are required to change their habits and use the new system.
- *Don't* expect methodologies to have much to say about change and commitment.

THE A B C STAGES

As you develop your systems, you should expect to progress through three stages. *Building* is, of course, one stage. I call the other two stages *activation* (preceding building) and *consolidation* (after building) (see Figure 16.2).

Activation means *getting started*. The most influential sales and marketing people must be actively involved in and committed to systems development from the outset. They must begin to understand what the systems will mean. After all, their staff will be using the systems.

Building means *getting results*. This inevitably involves more technical people. Individuals must be provided with the skills and resources to build the systems on time, on budget and to the required quality. They may need support from methodologies for project management, design review, package selection, system testing and user training.

Consolidation means *getting better results*. This phase involves the most people. It requires adjusting the organisation's internal environment to obtain lasting results. New planning processes are needed. Education and internal communications must ensure that people understand the rationale behind the systems. Job content and organisation structure must be adjusted. Monitoring and reporting must be made to happen: often they rely upon people's cooperation to work. Systems management and staff may need to work in a different way.

AN EXAMPLE OF THE ABC STAGES

The following example shows how these stages may apply to a typical consumer products company.

1 *Activation*. At first, marketing managers are doing all their analysis and reporting without computers. Hard copies of market research tabulations are available, on request, and huge piles of computer print-outs containing sales reports are produced monthly. A market researcher, for example Nielsen, introduces the idea of supplying its data through on-line access. One marketing group accepts the researcher's offer on a trial basis. This is the marketing department's first exposure to on-line data. The results are sufficiently positive to convince other marketing managers to use the system.
2 *Building*
   (a) *Automation*. Individual marketing managers acquire personal computers to support their needs. These are used on a stand-alone basis and data from other systems either has to be keyed into them manually or requires time-consuming help from DP staff.

	Activation	Building	Consolidation
Tasks	Corporate and business development plans Change impact assessment Cost – benefit analysis IT action plan	User requirements Functional design Technical specification Implementation	Refresher training Maintenance
End products	Evaluation report Plans and budgets Actively involved users	Fully tested system Planned campaigns Trained users	Actively used systems Successful campaigns Growing confidence
Benefits	Risks and rewards identified Management-led agenda	Quality systems on-time and on-budget	More revenue for less cost

Figure 16.2 Traditional and innovative management emphasis.

(b) *Fusion*. The need to fuse the data from several sources results in a bureau being selected to receive and store all the data. Access to the data is still via the different tools provided by the various research firms.

(c) *Integration*. The bureau's costs rapidly rise to the point where the company can cost-justify moving to an in-house computer. Direct feeds to the in-house system are added. A package selection study is initiated to choose a single set of end-user tools.

3 *Consolidation*. More and more marketing managers become proficient in using the system. They recognise the need to download data into spreadsheets on PCs. This capability is added by the systems group. An understanding of how to use the systems is instilled throughout the group.

IMPLEMENTATION PATHWAY

Progress with IT will be easiest in gradual and systematic steps. These steps must follow what I call the 'implementation pathway'. An example of such a pathway is set out in Table 16.1.

TAKING TIME TO LEARN THE LESSONS OF SUCCESS

The pathway in Table 16.1 has important milestones, at which tangible products are achieved (e.g. designs, programs). At each milestone, management must stop the project to take stock of the results, the successes and failures, before proceeding.

The most successful use of IT always follows such a systematic plan. It is essential to understand the complex, multidimensional development process.

You have to be willing to take time, learn from experience, and apply the lessons to make things better in the future. Phasing projects, to allow for regular reviews, enables performance to be assessed, and future plans to be adjusted as necessary.

Starting with a familiar focus helps allay the anxieties which invariably accompany any significant innovation. That is why it is usually desirable to begin with basic tactical automation. Confidence gained in this helps build an IT infrastructure and climate tuned to marketing and sales needs.

Successful IT users initiate organisational and cultural changes, as well as building systems, to ensure that the IT 'backbone' is exploited to its full potential. These are shown under the 'strategy' heading in the table.

Table 16.1 Implementation pathway

Stage	Strategy	Marketing and sales	Systems
1 *Activate*	Sharpen vision, consolidate goals and communicate internally Assess personnel needs, change impact and milestones	Prepare preliminary marketing costs and campaign plans	Assess needs for information and functions, technology basis plus costs, resources
2 *Build* (a) *Automation*	Determine goals of automation and communicate them internally	Refine marketing plans and finalise any marketing budgets	Select software, design and build systems Train users Offer limited support
(b) *Fusion*	Assess success of automation Determine fusion goals and communicate them internally	Develop coordinated campaign plans and extend budget	Build master database and put feeders in place Extend training and support
(c) *Integration*	Assess success of fusion Determine integration goals and communicate them internally	Refine marketing processes Extend budget further	Build the links between the integrated parts Extend training and support
3 *Consolidate*	Assess success Adjust jobs and organisation Improve internal communications	Strengthen planning process Improve monitoring and reporting	Improve training and support Refine systems Strengthen systems management

CONFIDENCE

Success breeds confidence in technology. This in turn stimulates further success and greater confidence. But confidence will not build itself, it requires a passion for excellence, a ruthless honesty and an ability to communicate.

Excellence is not common or easy. The history of IT is littered with failures brought about by overestimating what can be accomplished and underestimating long-term consequences.

Technology avoidance is often the result of past disasters. An objective and honest approach to existing systems is essential if confidence is to be gained for future systems.

Lack of confidence also results from the fears and uncertainties surrounding the impact of the technology. Watch out for compliance and going through the motions. Also beware of exaggerated results and bargaining for resources to suit personal ambitions and vested interests.

Pilots or prototypes can help to build confidence. Give users the opportunity to achieve tangible successes, even on a small scale, and obtain evidence that practical benefits can be achieved.

Conversely, allowing managers to get excited about and committed to systems that cannot be implemented is a recipe for disaster. The needs of enthusiasm sown by a system that subsequently fails will only grow into disillusionment and despair.

Technical excellence is a prerequisite for establishing confidence. Effectiveness audits can help. These elicit candid opinions from management and staff on the ability of the IT infrastructure (systems and support services) to meet current and future needs. Through interviews, discussion groups and the use of questionnaires, points of view on strengths and weaknesses can be collated, and form the starting-point for the next round of planning.

Finally, complacency can be one of the biggest threats to making the most of IT. After a system has been implemented, the attention and organisational priority generated by the development process often subsides. This leads to demotivation of those directly involved.

The end of the building stage is like the end of the honeymoon. For users, the novelty of doing something in a new and better way can fade. People forget, or never knew what happened before. Setting milestones, using effectiveness reviews and updating plans are essential to maintain momentum and enthusiasm. Organisations must continually strive to keep improving their systems. Without this effort, they will stand still, and fall behind their competitors.

WHO SHOULD PARTICIPATE INITIALLY?

Consensus is necessary for confidence to be widespread. There has to be a common purpose among managers who need information, staff who use systems, and DP managers and staff. Of all these, the seldom appreciated DP managers and staff are perhaps the most important. However, their input alone is not sufficient.

One way to obtain consensus is by encouraging the DP manager to work closely with the management group in marketing and sales. Active participation by experienced managers is necessary. For the majority of companies this usually takes the form of a steering group, which guides the development by setting priorities for applications, settling disputes and agreeing investment levels.

Typically a steering group is chaired by an impartial senior executive. Membership includes senior managers of each sales and marketing unit (e.g. all major product groups, advertising, direct marketing, telemarketing, all major sales territories).

The continuity of the group is important. It should continue to operate after the first round of planning is complete, to approve the activation of major projects, and to ensure adequate management and user commitment and involvement. It should monitor the progress of projects, approve exceptions and re-prioritisation, and be on the lookout for new opportunities.

QUESTIONS

1	When should a company innovate to ensure success? (a) first in its market sector (b) second in its sector (c) last in its sector.	☐
2	Do you have a policy for exploiting IT?	☐
3	Does your company have long-term IT objectives (i.e. does it have a clear idea of the systems it expects to build after those being used now become obsolete?)	☐
4	How strongly does IT figure in the marketing and sales strategy for your company? (a) very much (b) a little (c) IT is not mentioned.	☐

5 List the five key IT developments in your industry over the past ten years. How did your company react to them?
(a) embraced them all immediately
(b) dismissed some initially as of minor significance
(c) dismissed most or all.

6 Do your systems fail to reflect the business priorities you have established?

7 Is your DP department stuck with an increasing maintenance backlog?

Activating Your Organisation

We know what happens to people who stay in the middle of the road. They get run over.

Aneurin Bevan (1953)

Only 5 per cent of the people reading this book will develop a sales and marketing system in the next 12 months. When you put down the book and return to your office, all sorts of interesting opportunities involving earning money will crop up. Your interest in medium- to long-term projects will get shuffled to the bottom of the pack.

At a recent conference on sales and marketing systems I carried out a survey of people's aspirations regarding systems. There was a huge gulf between board directors and middle management regarding the urgency of acquiring systems. Whereas 75 per cent of middle managers felt something had to be done within 12 months, only 44 per cent of directors felt the same. The majority of directors thought that a decision could be postponed to next year or later.

Many middle managers who need systems are without the budgets to build them. As a consequence, they run small-scale pilots. The outcomes of these underfunded pilots are often perceived as failures, and consequently the required investment in sales and marketing systems is permanently postponed.

ACTIVE CONSIDERATION

So, if you are considering developing information systems, do not delay active consideration of how to proceed. Nothing is more likely to fail than indecisive dabbling with information systems.

Please note the phrase 'active consideration'. I am not suggesting that information systems are advantageous to every company or that they represent a panacea. Nor am I suggesting that the bigger and more expensive the system the more profitable it will make you. On the contrary, you may benefit most from having a very small, simple system. The point is that you need to decide actively what you need and how to get it.

Think about how systems have been introduced into your organisation, and describe which ones were actively introduced and which ones passively:

- *active* introduction is planned, with involvement from users and decision makers
- *passive* introduction just happens, systems that are probably the creation of some boffin seem to creep up on you from nowhere.

Which were successful? In most cases, those actively introduced were the successes.

I call the early stage of introducing systems the 'activation stage'. This is when the most important decisions are made. Often this is also the time when sales and marketing managers say 'yes' to the opportunities presented by their technical colleagues, without consulting the six honest servingmen – what? who? when? where? why? how? – and the seventh (which Kipling missed): how much?

Key questions for active consideration are:

- What opportunities can IT provide today, where is it going tomorrow and who will create this vision?
- How will management become involved?
- How much change will be needed, how readily can change be made and who will be responsible for the changes?
- How much will it cost and why should the investment be made?
- What is the implementation pathway, where are the priority areas and when will the milestones be reached?

It is clear that dealing with these questions will involve a lot of people and time. One person dedicated to the job may need anything from three weeks to three months. The work will involve:

- consulting people
- reading documents
- assessing requirements, benefits and priorities
- matching requirements to what is feasible
- producing a final document.

Many companies employ outside consultancies because tying up internal resources is not a viable option, and/or they do not have the in-house skills.

CREATING THE CLIMATE FOR INNOVATION

Marketing and sales directors and managers must become dissatisfied with the status quo for innovation to succeed. They must take the lead, in the activation stage, because the decisions being taken are too important to leave to DP staff.

This transformation must ultimately be acted out at all levels of the sales and marketing organisation. Directors must help managers build the knowledge base needed to guide the 'creative destruction' of the traditional DP approach.

Many general managers are already being told they must take a quantum leap into 'new technology'. Yet the aura of importance attached to IT can be the very reason why they find it hard to get involved.

Overexaggeration has led to disillusion and resistance. Technical advances are accompanied by media exposure, debate, high-pressure sales, ivory tower dreaming – and deep dread! The chorus from TV, press, conferences, seminars and books has shouted out the benefits of IT. The practical issues, however, have been oversimplified. IT is falsely presented as the easy panacea to business problems. In this situation, management are required to choose from a bewildering array of hardware and software, which often threatens to fragment or conflict with systems already in place, and cause integration problems that were unheard of a decade ago.

There is an unprecedented need for IT demystification programmes in all sales and marketing organisations today. These programmes will take many forms. They will include executive education (with a strong external view); sponsored research (to look for best practices); examination of industry and technology trends. The objectives are to reinforce new visions and signal the desire to innovate with new approaches, and to provide the organisation with the knowledge it needs to begin redirecting itself. Once the knowledge base is sufficient, the focus can shift to the problems of building new systems.

CASE EXAMPLE – CITIBANK

When Citibank first embarked on its electronic banking strategy several years ago, it undertook a radical move: it reversed its technocratic approach to computing, in order to broaden the base of people who could deal with information technology. Technical departments were broken up and assigned to lines of business. Standards for vendors were rescinded. The approach in general was to 'let a thousand flowers bloom'. As a result of this strategy, technology became everyone's problem. Instead of deferring decisions to technocrats in remote parts of the bank, the people responsible for new products and service levels were required to deal directly with technology. This radical move put Citibank ahead of the pack in terms of profitability, market share and development of technology-based services.

CASE EXAMPLE – FRITO-LAY

For Frito-Lay Inc., in the mid–1980s, external developments in the capture of market data by store scanners, and distribution of data by hand-held sales computers, led to a much richer view of the retail environment. Furthermore, scanner panels offered the potential for in-depth analysis of consumer behaviour through consumption and response to marketing programmes. These systems could increase the available market data by several orders of magnitude.

This data explosion arrived at a time when the brand groups had numerous things to do. They were barely on top of the existing data when the new data arrived. They decided on an integrated approach. They also recognised that:

- Integration is the key to economics. The operation of the business generates a large number of small transactions. Hence computers are vital to running the business. To provide the necessary services at a reasonable cost, an integrated system of hardware and software is essential, with network communications to achieve the integration.
- Leadership is the key to integration. The management services group must have the power to say: 'We are going this way. You may go that way, but we are going this way.'
- Vision is the key to leadership. To lead successfully, a clear vision of the future marketing, sales and computing environments are necessary, along with a view of their impact on the practice of management. Execution of this vision involves selecting and managing people, devising appropriate processes and controls, developing the technical architecture and choosing the appropriate funding strategy.

CREATING NEW VISIONS

New visions act as beacons to the future, guiding the organisation and its systems builders. An important question that often goes begging is 'who should develop the vision?'

Over the years, various devices, such as DP steering committees, have been invented to provide user input and guidance to IT activities. I find these devices increasingly inadequate. They tend to reinforce the status quo and stifle vision.

Usually only one individual is able to coordinate these ideas and create a coherent vision. Visionaries need a strong mental picture of what they believe to be the goal and an ability to express the vision in simple terms.

Vision is not a gift. It requires hard work, observation of other organisations (both competitors and in other industries), and the creation of a composite blueprint for one's own organisation.

Visionaries need to be managed. They have a special role, rather like that of the architect. And like the architect, marketing visionaries can create 'carbuncles' from time to time. Sometimes they make waves so violently that the only course open is to remove them.

The risks of mismanaging visionaries are high. In one company (who must remain nameless) the 'visionary' marketing manager was expected by directors to persuade his colleagues to accept his vision, without any clear signals coming from the directors themselves that they accepted it. When his colleagues failed to accept his proposal, the directors made him responsible for pushing through the change anyway. He pressed ahead, upset many colleagues on the way, and eventually left the company. Later, the Business Development director suggested an identical approach to the visionary, for the same reasons. Although *he* was not a visionary, he had authority and leadership skills. The vision was sanctioned. This was partly due to the different power bases of the two executives, but primarily because the director listened and responded to the other 'non-visionary' managers.

MULTIDISCIPLINARY TEAMS

The situation in sales and marketing today is strikingly similar to a situation that arose more than 50 years ago, at the outset of the Second World War. We had entered a new chapter in the history of warfare, when transportation and communication technologies redefined traditional boundaries, opening up global rather than regional theatres of combat. The first-time combination of air, amphibious and ground weapons signalled the need for a new approach to battle management. However, such a war had never been fought before, so there were no rules to fall back on.

One effective approach was the creation of multidisciplinary teams – economists, psychologists, physicists, soldiers and so on – who learned how to work together to solve problems. These teams were responsible for the success of the North Atlantic convoys, the defeat of the German U-boats, and for developing a new science of modern warfare. The potential members of a multidisciplinary team are shown in Figure 17.1. Each member of the team has specific tasks to carry out.

The multidisciplinary team concept can be aptly applied to businesses today, bringing a diverse base of knowledge to bear on systems and reorganisation issues.

For such teams to work, however, they must be allowed to operate outside the traditional functional hierarchies. Typical DP committees simply perpetuate the inflexible bureaucratic approach. The following disciplines are fundamental to this approach:

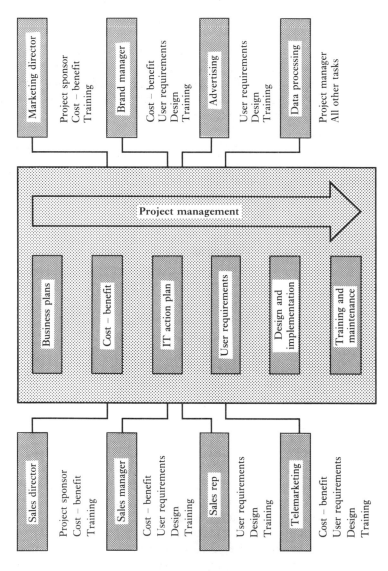

Figure 17.1 System change options after review.

- *Customer relations*. The team must be able to examine the relationship between customers and the products/services. Conducting a survey is a particularly effective way of understanding the shifting strengths and weaknesses that creep into customer relationships.
- *Process and structure*. The team must understand the sales and marketing process, and the organisation responsible for performing it.
- *Technology*. The team must understand existing and emerging technologies, and how they are being used by other companies.
- *Human resources*. The team must understand the attitudes and values of the existing workforce, in particular their ability to adopt changes, along with the need for cultural changes and new skills development.

External consultants can help. My company was invited by a major organisation to help develop the new business strategies, systems, training and organisation needed to compete in the 1990s. Their old way of operating was failing, and customer dissatisfaction was high. A multidisciplinary team was assembled, including:

- product marketing (in-house)
- statistics and research (consultant)
- advertising (both in-house and agency staff)
- sales (in-house)
- accounting (consultant and in-house)
- information technology (consultants and in-house)
- organisational psychologist (consultant).

The team approach was successful – the company has reversed its declining customer relationship and is growing rapidly.

LEADERSHIP

Teamwork is essential, but it is not a substitute for leadership. Leaders take the available resources – human, technical and financial – and allocate them, imaginatively yet wisely. They should not spread them out evenly, like butter on bread – that's what bureaucrats do!

A leader must strive to create shared 'ownership' of strategic visions. A charismatic leader can take a company to the pinnacles of profitability; one who has lost his or her nerve or vision could lead the same company to disaster.

A deep understanding of the importance of IT is vital, and a successful leader will ensure that:

- there is a clear Business Development Plan, or Sales and Marketing Plan
- directors and senior managers understand the impact and practicalities of building new systems
- general managers know how IT currently contributes to the business.

Figure 17.1 shows an analysis of the main revenue streams of one company which was considering how to use IT. These revenue streams were referred to in the business plan and were familiar to the Board. The IT director decided to show his systems plans on the same diagram: field sales systems, telemarketing etc. The board was readily able to understand the systems plans in this format, because they were presented in a way that linked with the business plan.

BUSINESS DEVELOPMENT PLANS/SALES AND MARKETING PLANS

Ideas and enthusiasm that come from the grassroots are important in many projects, but they are likely to fizzle out unless they are nurtured and encouraged from above. Unless the board backs the systems projects because they support business objectives and strategy, they will not receive the sustained backing that they need.

So, to plan systems, Business Development Plans, or Sales and Marketing Plans, are vital. Without them, organisations will pursue diverse systems opportunities with inadequate resources and conflicting rationales.

Many DP managers complain that they do not have access to such plans. Others justifiably point out that they have never seen what they would call a marketing or sales plan. While not every DP manager has perfect business judgement, it is true to say that many organisations routinely publish an annual Business Development or Sales and Marketing Plan, but the document is not taken seriously and may even be regarded as an irrelevant waste of time.

Often companies will need to prepare Business Development Plans *before* they start to investigate systems. Such plans should take account of competitor and peer IT usage, and industry trends, and assess how the company compares with the competition and 'best practice'. Only then can it map the business strategy and priorities onto the information needed to support them.

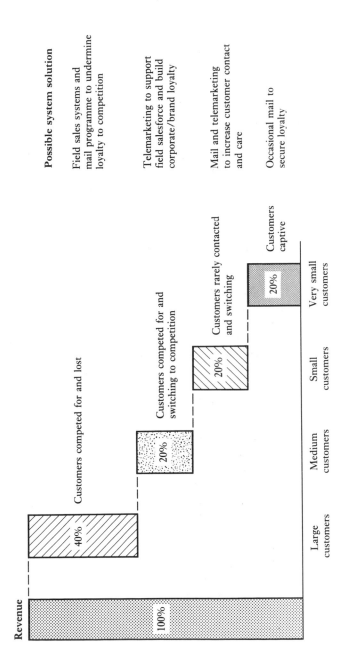

Figure 17.2 Business strategy needs to be reviewed first in order to identify possible systems solutions.

CHANGE IMPACT ASSESSMENT

The changes that computerisation will bring about must be carefully assessed before any commitments are made. Failure to assess the impact can lead to abuse, neglect, under-resourcing, lack of use, rejection by users, punishment of the innocent and promotion of the uninvolved.

Most readers will easily recognise or even identify with these issues. Managers wanting to adopt a new system should ask themselves:

- Am I ready for adoption?
- Who is willing to take care of the information systems?
- Who wants the information systems?
- How will everyone else react?
- Am I capable of looking after the systems?
- Will I be sufficiently disciplined?
- Do I know how to get the best out of systems?
- Am I organised to take care of systems?
- Do I have all the resources and equipment necessary?

Sadly, in many cases those adopting the systems only pay lip service to the success factors. The most important elements are leadership, shared vision and values, and top level commitment.

In most companies, particularly the more conservative ones, the status quo will be disrupted by the new systems. Users and providers of marketing and sales systems must be consulted. The result of consultation will be a presentation to senior management, focusing their attention on problems and solutions. Often the use of a chart similar to Figure 17.3 is useful in presenting the options to management.

The need to improve should be defined. The areas covered will include:

- planning methods used for identifying opportunities and setting allowable campaign costs (e.g. expense to revenue targets vs breakeven targets)
- budgeting methods for allocating funds from existing advertising and sales promotion budgets
- key performance indicators (e.g. expense to revenue ratio (E/R), lead conversion rate, campaign response rate, contribution per campaign)
- reporting: the format of reports used to present the results and to present future plans, and some consistency in the format and content of plans that are produced within the different product sectors.

The ability to improve must be assessed. This includes:

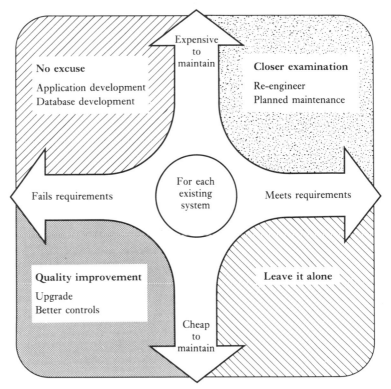

Figure 17.3 **A multidisciplinary team is needed for the project to succeed.**

- systems problems (perceived and actual) and ability to solve them
- organisational resistance (e.g. data ownership, sales feedback) and methods of overcoming them (e.g. clarification of roles and responsibilities, internal communications)
- knowledge and skills: i.e. their dissemination among users and specialists, and methods for educating, training and supporting them (e.g. help desk).

Based on such an assessment, strategies for improvement need to be formulated. This involves:

- setting the right direction (management focus groups, competitive benchmarking, campaign effectiveness audit, business priority workshops, benefits assessments)
- creating the climate for improvement (roles and responsibilities task force, information ownership assessment, change agent identification, vision and awareness, project management processes)

- knowledge transfer (training needs, management development, messages for internal communication, ideas forum)
- technology assimilation (methods and procedures, skills maintenance, support and help).

COST-BENEFIT APPRAISAL

The introduction of systems for marketing and selling represents an important investment decision for which there are a limited number of real-world examples. It is important to examine the benefits and estimate the costs before deciding to move to implementation.

Costs are notoriously difficult to estimate accurately. There are two main techniques available for estimating. The first is to make comparisons with other actual developments, where similar systems have been built. Consulting firms can often provide a good source of such estimates, since they maintain databases of cost information specifically for estimating purposes. The second technique is to subdivide the system into its component parts, and to estimate the component costs and the cost of assembling them.

Benefits, too, are difficult to estimate. A few companies have used IT to help *redefine the fundamentals* of their enterprise and the marketplace in which they operate. This bold step is, I must say, rare and most difficult to justify. Nonetheless, a few examples – American airlines, American hospitals – demonstrate the huge payoff that such developments can obtain.

Most examples of hard, quantitative benefits come from traditional *cost-saving* automation applications. Profit Improvement Planning methods, available from many accounting firms and consultants, can help to quantify these benefits and identify the areas that will have the greatest potential yield. This can be especially useful when trying to set priorities.

A substantial range of companies are also reporting the achievement of *revenue increases* from better customer service, and from more targeted, more responsive communications.

The benefits of *better management decisions* resulting from EIS and DSS are sometimes cited as justifying the IT investment.

CASE EXAMPLE – HEWLETT-PACKARD

Four challenges drove Hewlett-Packard to consider the benefits of information systems:

- cost per order dollar was rising

- industry growth was slowing
- competition was increasing
- complex products were getting harder to sell.

To measure benefits, three pilot test groups were established. A total of 130 reps in New Jersey, Illinois and Colorado were issued with information systems. Measurements were made of time usage before and after they received the systems. Care was taken to assemble control groups in each area as well, to calibrate any potential Hawthorne effects in the quantitative results.

The key measure, customer contact time, increased from 26 per cent to 33 per cent. Where did the time come from? The information helped the reps stay on the road and keep out of the office. They could access information themselves, remotely, outside the office. They could communicate electronically, reducing the need for meetings. This meant fewer trips back and forth to the office, and less time lost from *ad hoc* meetings and chitchat.

QUESTIONS

1
From what sources are IT applications initiated within your organisation?
(a) top management/directors
(b) senior and middle management
(c) systems management
(d) specific research projects
(e) corporate/strategic planning process
(f) external advisors.

2
How fast do new ideas move through your corporate hierarchy from junior management to board level?
(a) within weeks
(b) witnin months
(c) it takes years.

3
Is there a clear, formal structure for gathering, testing and assessing new ideas. Does everyone know what that structure is?

4
When did you last carry out an opportunities audit?
(a) within the past six months
(b) within the past two years
(c) what's an opportunities audit?

5 What proportion of managers in sales and marketing have been involved in workshops to identify IT opportunities?
(a) over half
(b) less than half
(c) less than 10 per cent
(d) none.

6 How would you describe the degree of commitment among ordinary employees to your existing systems?
(a) high
(b) modest
(c) low
(d) nil.

7 How hard does management try to involve employees in improving systems?
(a) very hard
(b) moderately
(c) not at all.

Building the Systems

I like work; it fascinates me. I can sit and look at it for hours.

Jerome K. Jerome (1889)

The sales director of a company I worked for several years ago was prone to unannounced walkabouts, much to the dismay of his staff. On one occasion he was passing through the computer department, and noticed a long-haired, bearded, casually dressed young man apparently staring into space and quite oblivious of his surroundings. After observing this phenomenon for several minutes, the director asked me who the young man was and what he was supposed to be doing.

'He's a programmer,' came my reply, 'and he's thinking about the system he's building.'

'Really?' said the director, 'well get rid of him and let him do his thinking on someone else's time.'

Although that incident occurred some years ago, it illustrates an attitude that persists today in spite of the much wider use of computers. However, today's marketing and sales managers have less excuse than our friend above.

Most sales and marketing managers lack confidence in the people they employ to build systems. They do not really understand what 'building' a system entails. They find the jargon difficult. On the other hand, the behaviour and work patterns of many computer staff have done little to improve their image, which I believe to be generally poor. Typically such staff are academically better qualified than their counterparts in other departments but are less experienced and have an inflated view of themselves, they are well paid but are more loyal to the computer department than to the organisation as a whole.

There is often a sneaking feeling that in this age of cheap computing power, we may not need these unwholesome computer staff for much longer. Theoretically, there is no reason why we as individuals could not be DIY computer technicians. However, just as we sensibly do not attempt open-heart surgery after reading the right books and watching television programmes, it is as well to recognise that, even at this much lower level, there is a background of knowledge, experience and skill that the average manager should not attempt to reproduce.

So, what are the jobs that computer technicians perform? An analogy with the building trade is helpful in distinguishing the nature of the different jobs in building a system.

- The building is conceived by an architect (equivalent to the systems architect, often a management consultant) in response to a request from potential users.
- The blueprints are drawn up by surveyors (the systems designer/analysts). They may seek guidance from technical specialists such as plumbers, electricians, structural engineers (telecommunications engineers, systems software engineers, database analysts, hardware specialists).
- The conversion of the blueprint into a building is the responsibility of the site manager (the project manager) who will determine and plan the building process to make the best use of resources and labour, and who will decide what tools and equipment are needed (computer-aided systems engineering tools, fourth generation languages, etc.).
- The work itself is done by craftspeople (the programmers) with assistance from specialists who carry out various finishing jobs (procedure writers, trainers).

Several types of computer jobs act as intermediaries between the source of computing power and the users and their problems. In particular, designers, analysts and programmers are specialist jobs that contribute to the building of systems. Some of the tasks that must be performed are described below.

PROJECT EVALUATION/SELECTION

First, the analyst must seek to establish whether the problem posed by management is amenable to solution by computer. To do this it is necessary to envisage the nature of the required systems. Business issues often need to be resolved here, in addition to any technical issues. Some typical issues that the conceptual design must address are:

- *Future direction*. What is the future impact of marketing strategy on customer acquisition, loyalty and retention, product development, etc., and how does this affect information needs? Do systems contribute to the achievement of the company's marketing objectives? Do they facilitate the sales plan?
- *Competition*. How does the organisation's use of computer-aided marketing and selling compare with that of specific competitors, or the industry as a whole?
- *Automation/applications*. What marketing or selling process needs to be automated? What information does management need to run the business effectively? Where are the greatest opportunities and what are the priorities?

- *Databases/fusion*. What are the critical information sources and how should the information be held?
- *Integration*. What is the business cycle and what are the information flows between the various parts of the business? How will marketing and sales interface with other corporate systems?
- *Technology*. What hardware, software, communications mix will best keep the organisation in line with long-term technology trends?
- *Costs and timescale*. What will it cost and how long will it take? Has enough time been allowed for the systems to be learned by users? Should investment be stepped or single point? Which parts of the system are cheap and which are expensive?
- *Resources*. Has management committed sufficient human and financial resources? Is there a suitable mechanism in place to make adjustments as necessary? Should resources be in-house or bureau?

ANALYSIS OF USER REQUIREMENTS

If the results of the selection are favourable, the analyst will, as a matter of professional pride, interview managers and staff about the current uses of information and processes, study the operation of existing systems and collect samples of existing documents.

Some commentators would argue that this is unnecessary and that, given the parameters of the business, it is perfectly possible to design a solution without reference to the operation of present procedures. After all, is not this the way in which successful general application packages are designed?

Such claims are invariably made by package suppliers, and it would be foolhardy of the users to select a solution without first having a qualified analyst become thoroughly familiar with the present operation, so that they may make an objective assessment of what is required.

Once requirements have been ascertained, a solution must be designed.

DATA/FUNCTIONAL DESIGN

Data is the raw fuel on which systems run. Unfortunately, the existing raw data within an organisation will not be in a suitable state for direct use by marketing or sales.

A design must be created for the information needed in the future. Data models should be developed as an aid to understanding the design. Accuracy of existing data must be evaluated, as well as its technical layout. The contents of files should be validated. Finally the sources of data and techniques for its enhancement need to be determined. These sources will include:

- data exchange between systems
- obtaining new data from customers and enquiries
- creating question banks from enquiries and surveys
- purchase from external databases
- deriving data by modelling or forecasting.

A 'data model' is a blueprint of the data that sales and marketing require. It sets out each item of data (called entities) and defines logical relationships between items. This logical data model structure then forms the backbone, onto which successively more detailed levels of information are attached.

The data model will be carried through to each individual application development project, thus ensuring consistency across the projects. The model usually consists of several different levels of detail.

There is the 'corporate data model', which is referenced by every application development project to see where areas of data overlap occur, and be used as the starting point for derivation of the 'application data models'. These are incorporated into the corporate data model, so that it continues to a 'live' model driving subsequent data development, and not merely an out-of-date view of how data requirements could have been coordinated.

Data modelling is a multi-stage iterative process.

1 The first stage, producing the 'business data model' of all sales and marketing systems, shows all entities that are relevant to all sales and marketing applications, as well as the key elements for each entity.
2 The next stage is for 'logical data models' of the applications to be developed by each application project. These will include data elements required to support the applications. These models will be merged into the data model, so that it continues to be a common representation of all data requirements. The logical design is then completed by using normalisation techniques.
3 This is then converted during physical design into a physical database design, based upon the database management system being used for the application. This takes account of traffic flows and access paths required.

The other aspect of the design is the functional design. Function charts or data flow diagrams are produced, showing the logic, input and output activities performed by the systems. Together with the data models these form the core of the data/functional design.

TECHNICAL DESIGN

Once the functional design is complete, and has been reviewed and agreed by users, the technical design must be prepared. This determines the way in which the systems will work. The elements of the technical design are:

- physical design of the database
- program/module design
- performance calculations to assess the feasibility of the design
- hardware and software design

There is a tendency for DP management to cling to old, familiar but outmoded technologies.

In banking, for example, new systems are being superimposed on layers of old systems, with each one adding costs on top of an infrastructure that was built in the early 1970s. They are institutionalising inefficiency, rather than rethinking what really needs to be done.

The infrastructure that is needed for the 1990s will be very different from that which sufficed in the 1970s and early 1980s. Much software in the past was not designed to cope with the complex, business-critical demands that now characterise marketing and sales requirements.

Getting rid of outdated technology and replacing it with facilities that will survive the 1990s is a tricky challenge that most companies will have to face at some stage. In many cases, the only solution is to throw the lot away and start again.

Such drastic action, although costly and traumatic, can be a blessing in disguise. An airline who got rid of their outmoded database, run by a third party, and began building systems round a relational database got an enormous gain. They have no marketing systems that pre-date 1988, and the speed and flexibility of the new systems, and the direct access they give end-users to the data, has revolutionised them.

How much should be spent? Recent surveys in the UK show that 3000 UK companies are spending over £1 million on IT. *Computing* has recently published figures showing total expenditure on IT in the UK (see Table 18.1).

In addition, approximately one-third of all expenditure is on staffing costs (about £5 billion in 1989). The most interesting observations are that:

- education and training are growing faster than all other expenses

Table 18.1   IT expenditure in the UK

	1987 £m	Growth %	1988 £m	Growth %	1989 £m
Education and training	138	60	221	41	312
Packaged applications	429	28	548	26	689
Other software/services	2380	22	2899	10	3186
Microcomputers	739	41	1039	8	1117
Minis/mainframes/datacomms	3543	19	4208	10	4648

Source: *Computing* (10 May 1990)

- hardware is rapidly declining in importance, but still dominates today's DP budget
- packaged software is outgrowing all other modes of software development.

PACKAGED SOFTWARE

A recent survey of UK businesses showed that three-quarters have computerised their client data and half have computerised their prospect data, and that the majority have used packages.

There has been an explosion in the number and the quality of software packages and services – over 100 'off-the-shelf' marketing software packages are now available in the UK. There are many variations between packages, both in the range of business needs addressed and in the method by which individual needs are satisfied. Package suppliers try to make their solution meet your needs by various means:

- letting users alter the packages to fit their individual needs by using 'set-up' utilities (normally the extent of such alterations is somewhat limited)
- offering a more extensive package 'tailoring' service
- allowing clients' technical staff to alter the package.

Most packages aim to be flexible and easy for non-technical people to use. Often one package will not provide all the flexibility needed, and so a solution involving two or more packages (e.g. a marketing database plus a spreadsheet) is the right answer. Sometimes information from other departments has to be merged with marketing data, and some packages offer the capability to merge such data directly, without the need to retype it. Or perhaps multiple locations have to be supported, again some packages offer answers to this requirement.

Packages should not be selected simply on the basis of suppliers' demonstrations. A systematic selection process is needed, to avoid the pitfalls. Table 18.2 shows the steps that I would recommend in undertaking a package evaluation exercise. I have set out alongside them some of the common pitfalls of missing out the steps.

Table 18.2 A package evaluation exercise

Step	Common pitfalls
1 Define your needs	Failure to discover the inadequacy of the proposed package
2 Identify the options	Too many products, resulting in a confusing selection process
3 Request for proposal (RFP)	Inability to distinguish the products due to the lack of standard criteria
4 Define selection rules	Failure to concentrate on the most important criteria
5 Evaluate	Failure to predict the system's costs and impact on your performance

Packages are important. They offer a relatively inexpensive, easy-to-use way of testing out computer technology. While they may not ultimately solve all your business needs, they provide a means of building confidence, without having to wait for DP to build their own solution.

SPECIFICATION AND PROGRAMMING

Having established the technical design, the analyst/programmers will produce a detailed specification that can be acted upon by more inexperienced programmers. This will show physical file layouts, structure charts for programs, definitions of controls, etc.

You may feel that it has taken a long time to convert your requirement to a form in which a computer program can be written. The process of systems analysis can be long and often laborious but, unpalatable and costly though it may be, my experience suggests that the number of problems encountered at the programming stage is inversely proportional to the amount of time devoted to requirements analysis and design.

This must be so. The programmer's task is to convert the specification into instructions that will run the computer. If any of those steps is imprecise, the effort to correct the 'bug' may be ten times greater than the effort saved on a skimpy design.

Finally, coding is the moment the programmer has been waiting for. The programmer will select a repertoire of computer instructions and commands that will carry out the functions of the program. In spite of the care taken, it is highly likely that something will go wrong because of mistakes in using commands, or through faulty logic in the design, or poor analysis of requirements.

WALKTHROUGHS AND TESTING

'Walkthroughs' are an important way of improving quality without huge costs and effort. There is nothing mysterious about a walkthrough, it is simply a group review of a specification or program, prior to live testing. To many systems analysts, the notion of spending an hour with users arguing about the specification seems to be a waste of time, or even an invasion of their privacy. However, walkthroughs are one of the most effective ways known to improve the quality of an information system.

The notion that analysts can decide for themselves the correctness of specifications, and that all errors can and should be ironed out by testing have proved expensive misconceptions. In contrast, walkthroughs have been found highly successful in producing reliable, bug-free systems.

Walkthroughs should be structured and relatively formal. We are all familiar with the 'informal' walkthrough, consisting of a quick huddle round some scribbling that has been produced on the back of an envelope. Inevitably errors and flaws are overlooked by the reviewers. Ideally the review ought to be characterised by:

- a long preparation time
- relatively complete and precise documentation
- critiques in detail produced quickly
- a sense of responsibility on the part of the reviewers.

It is very important to have a frank exchange of views at a walkthrough. One technique that helps this is to have only peers – equivalent grades – attend the walkthrough so that no one feels inhibited. As one analyst said: 'Every time my boss attends the walkthrough, I start worrying that he's keeping score in his little black book.'

If the walkthrough is successful, then a live test is called for. Live testing should be performed in several steps:

- determine the test for one computer operation, and the expected results, and then put it through its paces – check whether the expected results were achieved
- determine the test for all linked processes, and test them together
- have the users test the system, without help or supervision, to see if they can 'break' it.

PROJECT MANAGEMENT

The objectives of the building stage are deceptively simple: to produce quality systems, on time and within budget. Successful systems building does not happen by chance. It requires project management. This typically involves using structured methods for planning, organising and controlling work.

The image of project management seems to be inconsistent with that of the swashbuckling entrepreneur who is the hero of modern business. Tom Peters, the American management guru, has many times claimed that the problems of US companies in the 1970s were due to over reliance on management techniques. Senior directors of British companies can also be heard voicing their distrust of project management techniques, as being too rigid or cumbersome for their requirements.

It is undeniable that a project manager can suffer from an overemphasis on technique. Besides, traditional project managers, who are drawn largely from the data processing discipline, seem unlikely to join the entrepreneurial heroes of the 1990s. However, this is to miss the main point about project management.

A project is simply a piece of work with particular characteristics: an objective, a beginning and an end, and a series of linked unique activities in between. Viewed in this way, project management could well be regarded as an enabling mechanism that allows innovation and change to take place.

THE PROJECT MANAGER

There should be no second chance when you are implementing a system. You need to appoint a project manager whose career and future are 'on the line'. Many a system's success has been directly tied into the project manager's role. To succeed, the project manager needs to apply an up-to-date knowledge of the tools and techniques of project management.

In practice, many managers find themselves working on 'project teams' while simultaneously carrying out their official jobs. Companies are inclined to set up interdepartmental project teams to build systems. These teams will succeed only when they are under the management of one individual – the project manager.

In appointing the project manager, you should be careful to ensure that they have skills in the following areas:

- successful team building, knowing how to mix and match the skills and personalities of team members
- effective project planning, scheduling and schedule projection
- rigorous project budgeting, tracking and projecting

- keeping tight control of timescales and estimates to compiete
- managing problems and conflicts within the team and between the team and its sponsors.

Project management is about attitudes as much as about skills, techniques or procedures. At its simplest the project team is an *ad hoc* group brought together to achieve a given task. It is likely to be supported by a number of tools and techniques, such as critical path analysis, project management software, time and cost reporting. It certainly requires a wider range of skills than most line managers possess. For this reason, the right choice of project manager is the most important decision of the systems building stage.

PROJECT MANAGEMENT TECHNIQUES

Most system building aims to achieve multiple objectives. In Part I we proposed that three strategies should be implemented: automation, fusion and integration. Each strategy may have multiple objectives. For example, automation may involve field sales automation, telemarketing automation and brand manager automation. Such an undertaking should be split into multiple projects, so that expenditure can be aligned with objectives (see Figure 18.1).

Each project should be subdivided into smaller and smaller work units: stages into tasks . . . tasks into steps . . . until units of one to five person-days; effort are reached. For each task, there needs to be a plan available. This should be prepared at the conclusion of the preceding task.

The work needs to be organised at the outset, with clear definition of who is responsible for what. *User involvement must be clearly stated.* Throughout the task, control must be exerted to ensure that it stays on track. Finally, it needs to be formally concluded. The concluding step is the one at which quality control most comes into play. It is good practice to have a formal walkthrough of the result of each step.

The plan should show dates by which given tasks will be 100 per cent completed. I stress 100 per cent because there is a common tendency among technical people to cut corners, and say that 95 per cent complete is good enough.

How long do typical tasks take? While there are no fixed rules, one should aim for the following:

- high-level strategy   4–12 weeks
  - detailed project plan   4–12 weeks
  - user requirements/functional design   8–16 weeks
  - technical design   8–16 weeks

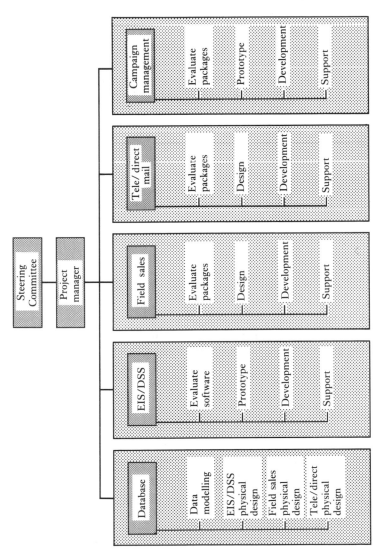

Figure 18.1 Project organisation.

- development (coding, testing)   12–24 weeks.

While the actual time taken depends on the level of resources committed to the work, these times are useful guidelines. If much less time is taken, it is unlikely that the work will be thorough enough. If more time is taken, the project will probably not maintain its direction or momentum.

If one is presented with larger project timescales than this, it is best to split the project into smaller, more manageable pieces. With package development, the timescales sometimes appear to be less. Be cautious – there may be hidden factors in the work that will eventually lengthen the timescale.

Tight progress monitoring (every week or fortnight) and regular assessments against milestones and budgets are essential to keep on track. Sometimes you will find there are continuous problems; for example, all tasks are 50 per cent over budget, no deliverables pass the user walk-through without major changes. The project manager has to take tough decisions: counselling his or her team on poor quality work, making adjustments to budgets and timescales to keep the project steering towards a known goal. Occasionally, the outcome of these reviews is to cancel the project – this may be better than to continue pouring money into a bottomless pit.

Suppliers are frequently difficult to manage. Penalty clauses in contracts may help to ensure that they keep to your deadlines. However, be careful that your penalties don't drive them out of business – to your mutual disadvantage. It is usually best to work in partnership with suppliers, and to ensure that they are committed to your project plan.

QUESTIONS

1
Do you have a 'systems architect'?
(a) yes, we have a competent, trusted, clear talking, clear thinking individual
(b) nobody suitable exists.

2
In building new systems, what does your company do?
(a) form multidisciplinary teams, with marketing and sales strongly represented
(b) make DP produce what marketing or sales says it needs
(c) let DP produce what it thinks marketing or sales should be using.

3 What sort of procedure do you use for selecting projects and defining user requirements?
(a) a systematic formal process
(b) informal methods
(c) we muddle through somehow.

4 How fully have your data requirements been defined?
(a) complete models exist
(b) we started modelling but never seemed to finish
(c) not defined.

5 Has the technical infrastructure in your company been defined
(a) complete formal definition exists
(b) it is all in the heads of our DP managers
(c) nothing has been defined.

6 How fully are you making use of available packaged software?
(a) we have reviewed what is available
(b) DP dislike packages and prefer to do everything themselves
(c) don't know.

7 How adequately tested are your systems before they go into live operation?
(a) very thoroughly tested
(b) poorly tested
(c) untested

8 Do top management obtain the most appropriate project managers to make IT a success?

Consolidating the Results

We trained very hard, but it seemed that every time we were beginning to form into teams, we would be reorganised. I was to learn later in life that we tended to react to any situation by reorganising, and a wonderful method it can be for creating the illusion of progress, while producing confusion, inefficiency and demoralisation.

Petronius (AD 66)

Sales and marketing thrive on change: correct? Change is certainly commonplace. One hears daily of major business initiatives such as product line extensions, brand repositioning, European market entry, salesforce expansion, channel development, and the introduction of total quality management or customer service programmes.

However, when it comes to implementing vital changes to information systems, sales and marketing directors and managers are slow and unimaginative, too concerned with short-term paybacks and still regard information systems as the province of financial management and computer specialists.

They cannot claim to be waiting for better technology to turn up. Though many improvements will be made in the next few years, there are few new rabbits to be pulled out of the technologist's hat. Most requirements can be met by existing technology.

Building the systems will not, of itself, guarantee success. Success depends on being able to change the rituals of people's everyday work so that the systems will be actively used.

As one head of systems explained it:

My job now has almost nothing to do with technology. It is about creating the right attitudes, understanding and commitment from the other directors. We need to build an appropriate culture and desire to innovate which can deliver the major impacts from IT. But this requires fundamental changes to how things have been done in the past and it is proving very difficult to achieve.

Every company has its own cultural heritage and aspirations. In order to be among the very successful users of IT in the 1990s, marketing and sales must understand how to create and sustain the right management and organisational environment needed to instil a culture of IT success. From the mass of articles now published on this topic, and from direct experience, a distinct framework for a desirable IT culture has emerged. The first thing that must be tackled is sharing power with users.

SHARING POWER WITH USERS

Should the DP manager or the users be in charge? Should there be a planning team or committee? Should the users of DP keep the data clean? How much 'hand holding' should DP provide?

There are no right answers. However, given the importance of getting the right people involved, roles and responsibilities must be sorted out.

The most common source of IT initiatives is from senior and middle management, not from directors and top managers, or DP managers and staff. To succeed, these individuals must be given a share of the power needed to proceed in developing systems.

There will be a natural tendency among IT managers to resist the granting of such power. They fear that putting line managers in charge of IT projects will cause repetition of the same mistakes as were made years ago. This attitude must be overcome, as it undermines the sense of ownership among users, and may even reduce the quality of the systems.

CASE EXAMPLE

'Alan' had retired from his overseas general management post years ago, and now found himself in the marketing department. He was horrified to find that his company had no in-house way of producing an attractive typeset document without going to great expense. The DP department had chosen a terminal, which could be used as a 1970s-style word-processor, which produced ASCII output that was sent via satellite to the world headquarters, where it would be made ready for a typesetter, and retransmitted by satellite. The resulting disk would then finally be presented to a typesetting machine.

Alan felt that this mess should have gone out years ago. So one lunch hour, he took a document round to the friendly Apple centre, scanned it into a Mac, titivated it up on Pagemaker, and took it back to marketing. Marketing bought a Mac and a scanner.

From time to time the luddites from the IT department would come and gaze open-mouthed over his shoulder, as he moulded the document deftly into a work of art. However, they came to the conclusion that anything so easy to use by a layman like Alan could not be a real computer, and got their revenge by refusing to allow the marketing department to buy another Mac.

The moral of this story is that the so-called 'information technology' departments still for the most part behave like renamed data processing shops, imbued with mainframe and minicomputer thinking. They pretend to have come to grips with the new technology that users demand, but are out of their element when faced with many PC-based sales and marketing applications. They still adhere slavishly to single-supplier standards that kill most applications, when a policy of horses for courses would do the job in hand cheaper and better. Users like Alan are intolerable irritants to these corporate bureaucrats.

THE HYBRID MANAGER

Until recently, the world of corporate computing could be readily divided into two broad groups: users and DP 'professionals'. Today that simple classification will not do. The 'hybrid' manager, an individual equally at home in the worlds of marketing and information technology, is emerging. Alan in our story above is an example.

Hybrid managers have a particularly important role to play in introducing new systems, because they get to the bottom of problems that other managers cannot reach. It is no secret that making a success of systems is not a simple process: every stage is a stumbling block, from setting legitimate business objectives, management sponsorship and proper systems specifications, through to effective development methodologies and user training.

Hybrid managers need three particular skills:

- technical competence
- organisational skills
- business confidence.

They are people of energy who have the competence to identify and remove barriers and deliver results. Usually it is easier for people with a marketing or sales background to switch than it is for DP people. Gaining capabilities on both sides of the marketing/computing divide does not make for a quiet life. Hybrid managers run the risk of being regarded as outsiders by both camps. They may be regarded as cowboys by the DP staff and as boffins by the marketing and sales people.

Sometimes, if difficulties become so great that it is impossible to implement systems using entirely in-house people, consultants can help.

PARTNERSHIPS

The importance of ensuring that the right commitment and behaviour permeates through all levels of the organisation is, possibly, the greatest challenge. Certainly it is the most multifaceted. It is also the most amenable to the application of specific techniques and methods.

To create harmony, senior management must understand the value and place of IT in marketing and selling. Technical specialists must gain a better appreciation of the marketing and sales departments for whom they provide a service. Such partnerships do not happen naturally or without effort. They are bedevilled by problems: splitting of responsibilities between the board, users, and technical specialists; anxieties created by fears that this split responsibility means nobody is fully in charge; and general negative perceptions between partners. Working together and training together will help break down these barriers to partnership.

An airline who built a major frequent flier programme considered partnership to be one of the most critical issues it had to tackle. Users had an appalling view of their technical colleagues and the technical people were rude and arrogant, which did not help matters. Eventually, a partnership agreement was drawn up, setting up the goals of working together and also the etiquettes to be followed to achieve a satisfactory relationship.

QUALITY MANAGEMENT PROGRAMME

A quality management programme is needed for the existing systems to deliver the capabilities that users expect. The programme will be an on-going exercise to improve quality. It has three aspects:

- data
- systems
- skills.

Standards need to be defined and specific objectives set in each of these areas. Each area should then be assigned to an individual manager, who must assess the resources necessary to meet the standards.

DATA QUALITY

Most companies are clearly rich in information about customers, prospects and third parties, and significant sums are spent gathering information. Unfortunately, as mentioned earlier, this costly information is frequently managed very badly.

I have found widespread dissatisfaction with data quality and confusion about who is responsible for its improvement. Users cannot have total commitment to the information unless it is complete, accurate and accessible. There is a danger that the database will degrade and the systems will fall into disrepute.

Existing data is rarely exploited properly for analysis and research. Results of surveys are 'owned' by individuals, even if they are of widespread relevance. Leads that surveys can identify are not generally made available to the salesforce.

A data quality programme improves the quality of the data available to meet business needs. Standards are needed in the following areas:

- *Completeness*. Data must be completely available where business needs justify its collection, maintenance and distribution.
- *Accuracy*. Data must be accurate and up-to-date where business needs justify its maintenance.
- *Availability/security*. Data should be available to all who have a (defined) right to know.

People should know their responsibilities. Users are responsible for certain types of data. A data quality manager should be appointed to be responsible for certain other data (e.g. third party data, surveys, code tables).

The actions taken by such a programme might include:

- performing a data audit to evaluate the completeness, accuracy and availability of existing data, and to recommend standards that should be set and steps that must be taken to meet those standards
- reviewing and documenting data definitions and codes
- establishing third party surveys for monitoring sales and marketing activities with third parties
- establishing a survey forum to identify future survey needs and to coordinate their fulfilment.

SYSTEMS QUALITY

Managers frequently express dissatisfaction with existing systems. They often complain about bad performance and poor applications design. They need to be 'hackers' to get what they need.

Delays in developing better systems can result in lost revenue opportunities and escalating sales costs. By using better systems, enquiries, prospects and leads, which currently command the indiscriminate attentions of the face-to-face salesforce, can be managed cost effectively – leaving salespeople free to chase business.

Systems quality improvement should aim to improve the quality of systems available to meet business needs. Standards need to be set in the following areas:

- *Requirements*. The requirements defined by users during development must be met.
- *Flexibility*. New requirements and changes in requirement should be implemented with a speed warranted by business needs.
- *Faults*. Bugs, downtime and other faults must be corrected with a speed that can be business justified.

New responsibilities may need to be established. Users should report systems quality problems promptly and accurately. DP must resolve problems. The systems quality manager must review problem resolution and arbitrate in disputes.

A programme of actions for improving systems quality may include:

- developing and implementing a system problem log, to be used for recording problems, their resolution and any backlog
- writing a systems maintenance plan for existing systems
- recruiting resources needed to maintain systems to required standards
- establishing a systems quality forum to oversee the resolution of systems problems.

ORGANISATION AND SKILLS QUALITY

The range of responsibilities covered by those in charge of the information systems can be very broad, including operational management of inbound and outbound telephone, and development and support of systems. While the wide scope of these functions commonly reflects the dynamism and enthusiasm of the manager responsible, it is inevitable that the information systems do not receive the depth of resources and attention that they deserve.

Skills quality improvement should aim to improve the skills available to exploit the information resources. Standards must be set regarding:

- *Users*. People must have the understanding and ability necessary to obtain the benefits that the information systems were planned to deliver.
- *Support*. For specialist functions, where users do not need to develop the specialist skills (e.g. statistics), support must be provided.

New responsibilities must be established. An action plan may include:

- preparing a skills, education and support plan, based on discussions with management on the extent and need for user skills and support skills

- providing a help desk
- learning sufficient 'end-user' computing skills to provide non-technical day-to-day support for users
- performing a biannual 'user satisfaction survey' for users of existing systems.

TRAINING

Few would now question that attitudes are changing and that training is becoming a higher profile business activity. It is no longer thought of as a cost rather than a benefit. However, when economic difficulties loom, and companies retrench, expenditure on training suffers.

Information systems training is particularly important. There must be well-planned education and training programmes to maintain a successful IT culture.

Many courses are available on the overall approach to marketing and selling, and many on computing techniques, but there are no public courses (other than those run by my company) aimed at sales and marketing information systems.

In my work with companies using computers, I have found them encountering many problems in managing the complex set of issues and working relationships between brand managers, sales management, store operations management, systems staff and a wide network of suppliers (agencies, print production, telemarketing, mailing and fulfilment houses).

The conclusion I have reached is that education must be tailored to the needs of each business, if the dramatic changes that computers can bring about are to be achieved for marketing and selling. An example of a syllabus for such training is set out in Table 19.1.

Despite the lip-service paid to the need for training, budgets and resources are often inadequate. This is especially true of informal training. IT managers rarely seem to make time available for informal on-the-job training for users. If a marketing manager reads something about IT and asks the DP manager a question about it over lunch, the marketing manager should not be made to regret asking the question. It is by these informal conversations that ideas and knowledge can 'drip feed' between DP and marketing.

As well as the informal 'drip feed' and the formal seminar, the following areas of communication are also important:

- regular informal presentations and demonstrations by colleagues and other divisions of your company
- research studies into competitors' use of IT

Table 19.1 Syllabus (example)

Using computers for Marketing and Selling: Computer Basics
Sources of expertise and techniques; costs and benefits of computers; how to manage computers from concept to benefit; the marketing cycle and its role in integrated systems.

Change Management
The team – recruiting, developing and keeping the hybrid team; what to look for; how to organise, manage and train them; deriving systems objectives from the marketing plan; creating the right climate; project management methods; understanding the culture and changing it; sustaining the computer approach by internal marketing (newsletters and workshops); politics and people.

Project Management
Project planning, scheduling and implementation; typical lead times; making the project plan happen; what to do if there are continuous problems; getting suppliers to work to your deadlines; helping suppliers organise themselves to work with your project plan; things to watch; how to allocate accountability and make it stick; supervisory skills; teamwork – leadership; presentations; interviewing skills; team member appraisal; time management; ensuring quality in a system.

Systems Planning
The marketing strategy and its computer implications; planning a programme of campaigns to achieve long- and short-term results; co-ordinating with other campaigns; using databases as information sources; customer/prospect targeting; budgeting; developing a spreadsheet to forecast and analyse options; using data in retail site planning.

Communications
Understanding media choice; agency briefing and egvaluation; dialogue planning; contact methods; response methods; follow-up and fulfilment.

Telemarketing
Telephone techniques; customer service; sales skills.

Analysis
Response analysis; model development; market research.

Databases
Lists – when and how to use them; typical costs.

- visits and study tours to users of similar systems
- workshops to identify opportunities and changing business requirements.

THE NEED FOR CHANGE MANAGEMENT

Finally, understanding the degree to which both one's customers and one's staff are change resistant is a vital part of instituting the right sort of changes to get results from information technology.

Too often the advice directors get from agencies about 'database marketing' fails to take proper account of the diverse needs and aspirations of customers and staff. Sometimes the changes that DP management attempt to implement simply will not satisfy those needs. In other cases, the proposed changes have little chance of success because nobody understands the rationale behind them, or worse, they do not *believe* that information systems will satisfy their needs.

If the needs of customers and staff are met, and seen to be met, the business will respond quickly and easily to the changes brought about by information systems.

Organisations themselves can also be rated as having generally high or low resistance to change. This distinction is significant because it dictates the ways in which organisations cope with systems-driven change. The Virgin Group of companies has been cited as a classic example of a low-change-resistant organisation. It is relatively young and decentralised, with a skilled mobile workforce and flat management structures. Everyone is rewarded according to the degree to which they stimulate or support innovation.

Financial service companies provide many examples of high-resistant organisations. One company spent hundreds of thousands identifying opportunities to use information systems to create demand for its insurance, unit trusts, pensions and other services, yet its marketing director resisted these opportunities, saying that the additional paper they would have to process would put too much strain on existing resources. (Fortunately that director has been released.)

There are significant differences between the two types of organisations. High resistant organisations may need to concentrate more on motivating their people and developing some of the characteristics of low-resistance organisations. Low-resistant companies may attempt too many changes too quickly and fall prone to idolatry of the senior managers, which is dangerous.

QUESTIONS

1 How often do top management visit the users of systems?
(a) daily
(b) weekly
(c) monthly
(d) once in a blue moon
(e) never.

2 Who do they talk to when they visit?
(a) staff at all levels
(b) supervisors and managers
(c) the DP manager only.

3 How much effort do top management put into reinforcing and developing people's pride in the systems?
(a) a lot
(b) very little
(c) none.

4 How closely can you identify the source of each problem that leads to a complaint about the systems?
(a) to a programming bug
(b) to an error in marketing or sales' specification
(c) to a change in business circumstances
(d) not at all.

5 How closely are patterns of complaints analysed?
(a) very closely
(b) moderately closely
(c) not at all.

6 What percentage of your staff would you estimate espouse the quality ethic with regard to systems?
(a) none
(b) over 25 per cent
(c) over 50 per cent
(d) over 90 per cent.

7 What proportion of your sales and marketing staff will resist the increased use of IT?
(a) all
(b) about half
(c) less than half.

8 In your company, where does responsibility for IT education and training rest?
(a) with the line managers
(b) with the DP department
(c) in personnel
(d) it's the employee's own problem.

9 How does your organisation teach management about the relevant IT subjects?
(a) by putting them in situations where they will learn on the job
(b) by sending them on internal courses and presentations
(c) by sending them out to conferences, exhibitions and seminars
(d) by sending them to visit IT sites in other companies
(e) presentation by systems suppliers
(f) it doesn't educate its managers.

10 How satisfactory are communications between senior management and IT personnel?
(a) clear, frequent communications
(b) occasional contacts
(c) what communications?

11 How often do top DP management personally contact aggrieved users?
(a) for every serious complaint
(b) for some serious complaints
(c) never.

12 What proportion of DP staff could tell you the markets and marketing objectives of the products that their systems serve?
(a) over 75 per cent
(b) over 25 per cent
(c) less than 25 per cent.

Part IV   Conclusion

Getting Help

The reasonable man adapts himself to the world. The unreasonable one persists in trying to adapt the world to himself. Therefore all progress depends on the unreasonable man.

George Bernard Shaw, Man and Superman *(1903)*

Why are there so many computer disasters? Suppliers are a common cause of unreasonable behaviour. Yet what is it reasonable to expect? Who can help determine what is reasonable?

The list of goofs is legion, with embarrassing contributions from hardware and software suppliers, advertising agencies, data processing bureaux and list brokers. Even if it seems that nothing that could possibly go wrong, some suppliers seem to go out of their way to invent a catastrophe of their own. Blame is often placed on the 'unscrupulous salesperson' or the 'incompetent analyst'. The result is often punishment of the innocent and promotion of the uninvolved.

WHAT GOES WRONG?

CASE EXAMPLE

A prestige car manufacturer employed a bureau to run its loyalty programme. They were disturbed to find that a successful second sale to a customer deleted details of the first sale, making it impossible to track the effectiveness of the programme. Worse still, repeat buyers were all being sent letters as first-time purchasers. When the bureau laser-printed hundreds of thousands of letters back to front, automatically enclosed them in window envelopes and then mailed them, that was the last straw. They decided to move in-house.

General management were blinded by science when they first attempted to computerise. They did not understand the jargon and they did not understand what the tools for containing and processing their information could do or how they did it. At first they chose a packaged software product for simplicity.

The system went down and they were paralysed. They had to buy in expensive maintenance. They then discovered that their packaged software program could not do what they wanted, without expensive modification to meet the real needs of the business.

Finally they chose to custom build a new system. A feasibility study was started.

They thought that their staff, coordinating with the DP staff, together with several contract programmers brought in by their advertising agency, would have sufficient understanding of their business and its information needs to construct the perfect system.

A recession set in. They had to change some aspects of the business to respond to the marketplace. This affected the viability of the custom system, which was being constructed on the premise of the pre-existing conditions. The system had to be altered in mid-construction.

The custom development became extremely expensive. The budget was overshot and the system was not even operational.

Then a fault was discovered in a software program – every time a letter was printed, the records were corrupted. This fault did not appear until six months after the system began operation. The contract programmers' warranty lasted only three months from acceptance after testing. Economic loss was specifically excluded from their contract, as was the cost of manual entry to correct errors – not to mention the loss of goodwill with customers.

This example raises three important questions:

- Do you need help to avoid the risks?
- How do you assess the risks?
- Who can help you avoid them?

DO YOU NEED HELP?

Sales and marketing directors and managers are often reluctant to seek assistance, especially in the computer field. This is largely because of three factors.

The first is credibility. A common fear is that seeking assistance might show up an inability to resolve the problem yourself. This fear should be weighed up against the risks of failure. Success requires paying attention to numerous technical details, and planning actions that have not previously been undertaken or are to be done in ways substantially different than the traditional methods. Perhaps a little outside expertise is valuable?

Second, there is the fear that the cost will be prohibitive. If, however, the work is divided into small discrete tasks, and advice is only sought where necessary, then you should be able to guarantee value for money.

Third, there is lack of knowledge of who can do what and who cannot do what. Broadly speaking, you require someone to help you arrive at the best systems solution to suit your needs and budgets. They should be able to define needs in simple, clear English, without insulting your intelligence. Like a doctor, their job is not to ask the patient 'what do you think is the matter with you?', but to enquire about symptoms, make various checks, diagnose any problems, prescribe a solution and stay with the patient until they are happy.

How do you assess the risks? This is one of the most important issues for sales and marketing managers to address, yet all too often they tend to ignore the risks. They often are in such a hurry to acquire systems, that they do so blindly and end up with costly equipment that actually hinders rather than helps.

RISK MANAGEMENT

People rarely buy the first cars off the production line for any new model. They know it is too risky. Yet they rarely apply the same caution to new information systems.

Risks stem from the numerous technical details, judgements and actions that are new to general management. Figure 20.1 shows some of the steps that must be taken to acquire an information system. The main rules for avoiding the risks at each step are shown in Table 20.1. These are part of the risk management methodology that my firm has developed for use on all sales and marketing systems projects.

For all the above areas, if the problem is complex, enlist the help of an outside advisor. But what help should you seek and when?

First, throughout the process you should seek input from someone with experience in sales and marketing systems. Because the topic is new, and the systems are unique, lack of experience in the area is both a handicap and a risk.

Then, when you start actively considering what to do, the *corporate strategy* or *business development plan* will have to be put into a form amenable for systems planning. During the *change impact assessment*, you may require assistance from someone who has experience with similar changes, or who has surveyed their impact on other companies. In the *cost-benefit evaluation* you may need help from a benefits analyst. Then, for the *action plan* you may want help from estimators and project planners.

When you start building, you will almost certainly need a project manager. You will also need one or more systems analyst(s) to define *user requirements*. For the *functional design*, skills in data modelling are often necessary. During *technical design* you need someone who knows what choices of software and hardware are available, and who can act as a judge in the selection process. During *implementation*, you need a good programming supervisor, good programmers and experience of testing.

Finally, you will require trainers and a maintenance team. So, what

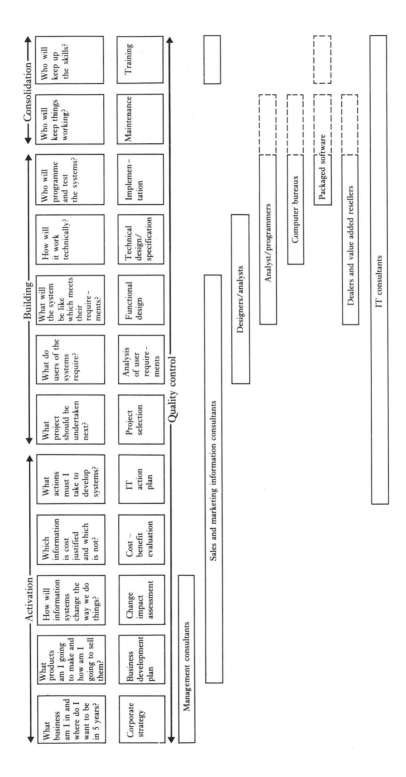

Figure 20.1 The road to integration.

Table 20.1   Risk avoidance

Step	Golden rules for avoiding risk
Corporate strategy	Priorities for the information systems must come directly from the strategy
Business development plan	The plan must contain details that will enable you to assess the impact of systems and estimate their benefits
Change impact assessment	The impact on other companies should be reviewed
	Some early benefits are needed to retain enthusiasm
Cost-benefit evaluation	Your current methods should be measured
	Benefits for other companies should be assessed
	Criticism of benefits estimates should be invited
IT action plan	Effort should be estimated in work-days
	A budget must be agreed
	Dates must be set for key tasks
Project selection	Management must have a high degree of confidence in the selected project
User requirements	A specification of requirements must be drawn up which the users understand and support as their own
Functional design	The design must be based on best practice, and must be well documented
Technical design	Reputable software and hardware must be selected, with plenty of room for expansion
	Shop around and get demonstrations
Implementation	Insist on professional programming and testing
Consolidation	Users must believe it is their system
	Operation of the system must be monitored to assure satisfaction
	There must be adequate training
	A maintenance contract should be signed
General	Directors and managers must believe in the systems and back their development
	Staffing must be assigned intelligently, with motivated individuals, and as much experience as possible
	The project must be managed professionally, with organised planning, documentation and reviews
	Communication must be open and frank at all times, with risks and issues promptly reported and quickly resolved
	Goals must be achievable and practical, with phased cost commitments

criteria should you use in selecting these people, and where should you look for help?

HOW BUSINESSES TRADITIONALLY SELECT ADVISORS

The factors involved in choosing an advisor in sales and marketing are periodically surveyed. They are shown in Table 20.2, in rank order of importance.

Table 20.2   Factors involved in choosing a sales and marketing advisor

Factor	Rank order
Past use	1
Cost/value for money	2
Their knowledge of my product area	3
Individual(s) within the company	4
Personal recommendation	5

The primacy of past use obviously does not mean that there is never any changing of suppliers. One consumer durables company said that it tended not to give major projects to a new supplier, but was happy to test it out on minor ones before giving it a chance to pitch for important business.

The problem for sales and marketing, however, is that in the past they have rarely, if ever, made any use of systems advisors, nor do they know what constitutes value for money.

So do businesses use systems advisors and, if so, how do they select them?

The majority of businesses do use external advisors for systems. In Europe, over £1000 million is spent annually on external advisors. Those who do not use them cite as reasons: use of internal facilities; policy to cover internal needs; facilities arranged centrally. Those who do, typically find them by word of mouth, from previous experience, from literature and the press.

The criteria used for selecting information systems advisors are shown (in order of importance) in Table 20.3.

Qualitative attributes that are considered important are: trustworthy, professional, responsible, creative, objective, innovative. Less desirable are external advisors who are leading-edge risk takers.

Table 20.3 Criteria used for selecting information systems advisors

Criterion	Rank order
Experienced/well-trained personnel	1
Ability to deliver/project management skills	2
Advanced information systems skills	3
Experience in my industry	4
Experience in my area of operation	5

WHERE SHOULD YOU LOOK FOR HELP?

There are several sources of information on where to get help:

- *DataPro* (published by McGraw-Hill) is the 'Bible' for reviews of what software is available. Other computer users' guides are also published but, to date, none cover sales and marketing specifically.
- Trade associations, such as the Chartered Institute of Marketing (CIM), the Association for Information Systems in Marketing and Sales (AIMS), the British Direct Marketing Association (BDMA), and the Advertising Association (AA) can provide lists of potential advisers.
- The trade press contains many articles describing case studies.

Most probably you will be directed to one of the following for advice:

- specialist consultants in sales and marketing information
- computer bureaux
- packaged software suppliers
- dealers, agents and value-added resellers
- advertising agencies
- IT consultants.

SPECIALIST CONSULTANTS

There are a growing number of specialist consultants (including my own firm) who offer help and advice on sales and marketing systems. This area is expanding rapidly, through defections from the IT consultancies and repositioning of bureaux. Services that are available include:

- *activation* – definition of strategies and business development plans, financial appraisals, media and product plans, new channel

organisation, sales targets and quotas, budgets and schedules, costs and benefits
- building systems – advice and analysis for user requirements, functional design, technical design, package selection and (sometimes) implementation
- consolidation – development and delivery of education programmes and documentation, design and execution of research programmes, analysis of customer databases, modelling for segmentation and scoring.

Such consultancies can be truly independent organisations, with no ties to or preferences for agencies, bureaux or suppliers of hardware and software. They are therefore useful to engage throughout the project.

BUREAUX

There are about 50 major sales and marketing computer bureaux in the UK, with mainframe computers. In addition, there are hundreds of smaller bureaux with personal computers.

Bureaux concentrate on building and maintaining databases. They typically offer low-cost solutions, and their quality tends to be somewhat cheap and cheerful.

Usually they offer a formula solution, which they modify a little to meet individual clients' requirements. They have probably done this hundreds of times. If what you require is their formula, then they are a cheap way of getting what you want.

Do not, however, expect them to help you much with strategy and planning, cost-benefit analysis or project management. Where functional and technical design are concerned, you can expect to get a formula. Bureaux rarely have any applications to offer, beyond simple direct mail. However, they can be a useful way of piloting a system, before committing major investment funds to its development.

PACKAGED SOFTWARE SUPPLIERS

There are over 100 packaged software suppliers in the UK and over 400 worldwide that specialise in sales and marketing systems.

Like the bureaux, they offer a formula. It is usually somewhat flexible, but you will soon run into its limits.

Most solutions to users' requirements will involve the use of two or more packages. (See Chapter 18 for advice on how to select packages.)

DEALERS, AGENTS AND VALUE-ADDED RESELLERS

If you want a complete solution, involving several packages and also hardware, there are hundreds of small dealers, agents and 'value-added resellers'. These companies mix and match software and hardware, and put together a system to meet users' requirements.

Like bureaux, do not expect them to help you much with strategy and planning, cost-benefit analysis, user requirements or functional design. However, they will help with technical design, installation, and also training and maintenance. Do be careful, however, to ensure that you sign a clear maintenance contract that offers what you want.

ADVERTISING AGENCIES

Most advertising agencies will offer to help develop systems. My experience is that 99 per cent of them subcontract the work. If they subcontract to a contract programmer (it happens frighteningly often) the consequences can be disastrous. Programmers are not normally skilled in strategy or planning, change impact assessment, cost-benefit analysis, user requirements, functional design, technical design, package selection, training, maintenance or project management. Therefore, my general advice is do not use them.

IT CONSULTANTS

Today there are many large, high-quality IT specialists operating worldwide. Their advice is sought by more than five out of ten British companies. Major firms include Andersen Consulting, CAP Gemini Sogeti, Hoskyns and Logica. All claim to provide better value for money in developing systems than in-house people.

How do they do this? Basically through concentrating on what they are good at: i.e. by training their people in the latest and best techniques, and by developing tools of their trade (Andersen Consulting had an annual internal expenditure programme of $250 million in 1989).

How can they be used? They can often provide assistance with strategy or planning, change impact assessment, cost-benefit analysis, user requirements, functional design, technical design, package selection, training, maintenance or project management. When systems are complex, they can provide particularly good support. They can also provide some of the best project managers available and, sometimes, good analysts and programmers.

The only words of warning are that in practice they lack marketing and sales skills – they often do a good deal of on-the-job learning (at the client's expense). Some may have a vested interest in recommending the biggest, most expensive, custom-built system they can persuade clients to accept, avoiding packaged solutions, and recommending that consulting staff continue throughout the project.

IN CONCLUSION

Finally, once you have decided what to do, do it. Avoid at all costs indecisive dabbling. Remember what happened to the Swiss watchmaking industry. They spent years complacently looking at the digital watch from Japan, until it suddenly swept across the world watch markets. Today they have reaped the consequences of indecision and inaction, and the 100,000 watch makers are now reduced to 10,000.

QUESTIONS

1 To what extent do you think the issues listed below are important to your organisation to obtain the most benefit from future IT investments?
(a) producing IT plans that clearly contribute to marketing and selling goals
(b) getting management to participate in IT planning and its implementation
(c) obtaining appropriate staff of high quality
(d) improving senior management understanding about IT potential
(e) improving the way in which IT projects are managed
(f) increasing management confidence that the IT function will deliver worthwhile results
(g) convincing top management that IT is not just an administrative necessity
(h) finding a way to gain management approval of projects where benefits are not easily quantified
(i) changing the attitudes and behaviour of IT personnel so that they are fully acceptable to senior management.

2 To what extent are you successful in resolving these issues?
(a) we can tackle them all without outside help
(b) we need specific help on certain issues
(c) we need help on all issues.

3
How effectively do you manage risks?
(a) we ignore risks and muddle through
(b) we tackle risks head-on
(c) we need outside help to avoid risks.

4
Do you know where to seek outside help?
(a) friends and colleagues can advise me
(b) trade associations are a useful source
(c) trade press can help
(d) don't know where to get help.

Glossary

Access time The time taken following instructions before reading from, or writing to, a storage location. The access time can vary from a few seconds for a magnetic tape to a few nanoseconds for the registers in the central processor.

Application Practical use to which the computer is put, such as direct mail, sales reporting or telemarketing.

Automatic call distributor (ACD) Telephone answering equipment that controls incoming calls, sends them to the available representatives, queues calls during busy periods, plays recorded messages or music to waiting callers and provides management reports on call activity.

Automatic dialler A device that allows the user to dial preprogrammed numbers by pushing a single button.

Batch processing Processing a quantity of data material, such as tape or disk files, as a single unit or batch. This may be done some time after delivery, as opposed to 'real-time' processing, in which items are processed as they arise. The time taken to process a large batch of data can be hours or even days.

Behavioural lists Data collected through questionnaires that gives such information as likes, dislikes, hobbies, etc.

Bureau An independent business offering such services as data processing, database management, mailshot selection.

Central processor Part of a computer system, consisting of an arithmetic unit, control unit and, sometimes, main memory.

Cleaning a list An updating process involving the removal of names or addresses that are no longer mailable.

Cluster analysis A statistical technique used to develop natural groupings of objects based on the relationships of the variables describing the objects. It is often used with census data to group neighbourhoods by type.

COBOL The most commonly used language for commercial computer applications.

Cold list A list that a broker or third party rents.

Contact strategy A predefined set of customer contacts designed to obtain maximum profit over an extended period of time.

Control The package, advertisement or offer that is used as a benchmark in future tests.

Conversion Making a prospect into a lead; or a lead into a buyer.

Conversion rate   The number of prospects needed to gain a lead; or number of leads needed to secure one buyer.

Cost per thousand   Common rate for list rentals.

Data   The information on which a computer operates, as opposed to the instructions in the program.

Database   An organised set of files providing a common pool of data for several or many users. Sharing data in one database helps maintain consistency between the 'facts' as seen by the different users.

Database management system (DBMS)   A type of software used for structuring, organising and managing databases. Some common examples are DB2, Oracle, Ingres.

Data entry   The actual entry of data into a computer, usually using a keyboard and screen.

Data preparation   The entry of data, and its validation, verification and correction.

Data transmission   The sending and receiving of data over a telephone or telecommunications line.

Deduplication   The removal of duplicate records from the in-house customer database.

Demographics   Social and economic information about people or groups of people, including age, income, education level, etc.

Disk   A thin flat circular plate coated with magnetic recording material. This can be a removable 'floppy disk' or a more permanent 'hard disk' on a PC or a 'disk pack' on a minicomputer or mainframe. Databases are commonly stored on disks, to provide more rapid access than tape.

File   An orderly collection of records maintained for reference, processing and updating.

Fourth generation language (4GL)   A more sophisticated language than third generation languages such as COBOL. Usually this means easier to use, more powerful and more productive for programmers.

Graphic user interface (GUI)   A type of software used to display data and programs in a form that the user will find easy to understand. Windows are widely used in GUIs.

Hardware   The physical equipment forming a computer system. The term has come into use to distinguish it from software.

Inbound telemarketing   Selling by telephone utilising incoming calls only.

Input   Data and programs fed into the computer memory before performing useful work on them.

Interface   A well-defined boundary between two systems. A simple example is the household plug and socket. In computer systems, data often needs to flow across such interfaces.

Language   A method of communicating between people and machines in which step-by-step instructions are written in the form of a program for subsequent processing.

Lead qualification The process of finding out more about a lead, to determine whether it qualifies for a sales visit or call.

List broker A service that brings a buyer (the list renter) and a seller (the list owner) together. The broker helps select lists, expedites receipt of lists and helps with merge-purge.

List source Origin of the names that appear on a mailing list.

List rental A one-time usage agreement between the owner of a list and the user. The owner may be paid a fee per thousand names rented, or a royalty fee to be agreed between the parties.

Mainframe The largest type of computer in common commercial use. Also the oldest.

Memory Part of the computer used to hold information in such a form that it can be accessed, used or understood.

Merge-purge A computer process whereby postal lists may be merged to facilitate postal code or mailsort sequencing and purged of duplicate and undesirable names.

Microcomputer The smallest type of computer, also known as a personal computer (PC). Also the newest, a product of the commercial manufacture of microchips, which became important in the late 1970s.

Minicomputer The middle size of computer, which grew in popularity in the 1970s. Used particularly for departmental applications and distributed uses.

Multiple regression analysis A statistical technique whereby a predictive formula is created linking a dependent variable (such as purchase value) to a series of variables (such as age, sex, occupation).

Networks Groups of computers that are connected together by a data transmission system.

Optical mark recognition (OMR) A data entry system in which information is formed by detecting the presence or absence of pen/pencil marks on a questionnaire or form.

Outbound telemarketing Sales made by outgoing telephone calls.

Output Information that is put out by a computer. It can take many different forms, either transitory, as on a visual display unit (VDU), or permanent, as in the case of printed documents.

Peripherals The hardware attached to the mainframe or minicomputer. Typical peripherals include VDUs and printers.

Program A sequence of instructions to a computer to carry out a given task. One program may be part of a larger program.

Psychographics Indicators of an individual's psychology. May include hobbies, habits, opinions and social roles.

Response rate The number of responses per thousand contacted.

Rollout A large mailing carried out if a test mailing is successful.

Score   A value calculated for an individual, which assesses characteristics such as propensity to purchase and creditworthiness. Often calculated using a multiple regression formula.

Segment   A subset of a market or list. The segment may be chosen on the basis of demographic, psychographic or other criteria.

Software   Programs, as opposed to hardware.

Systems analysis   The task of understanding and defining the way in which an existing business process works, or a new one might work, and specifying the computer system in a way that makes effective use of the available hardware and software facilities.

Tape   Magnetic tape used to store data.

Testing   A preliminary campaign to evaluate a product, advertisement or other element of the marketing mix.

Visual display unit (VDU)   A terminal device incorporating a screen and keyboard.

Index

TRIM, 84

Univariate analysis, 91
Univariate measure, 91
User interface, 20
User requirements, 179, 186

Value-added resellers, 211

Virtuous circle, 71, 77
Voice input, 20
VSAM, 146

Walkthroughs, 184
Willis, Gordon, 81
Windows, 98
Woolworth, Chester M., 93
Working day, typical, 127